OCEAN LINERS

BILL MILLER

MALLARD PRESS

Table of Contents

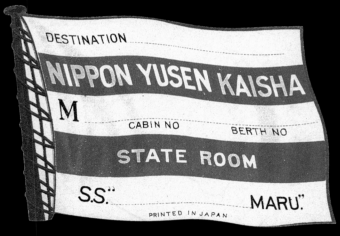

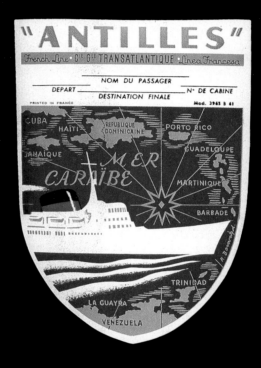

A FRIEDMAN GROUP BOOK

Published by MALLARD PRESS
An Imprint of BDD Promotional Book Company, Inc.
666 Fifth Avenue
New York, New York 10017

Mallard Press and its accompanying design and logo are trademarks
of BDD Promotional Book Company, Inc.

ISBN-0-792-45241-0

OCEAN LINERS: Travel on the Open Seas
was prepared and produced by
Michael Friedman Publishing Group, Inc.
15 West 26th Street
New York, New York 10010

Editor: Sharyn Rosart
Art Director: Robert W. Kosturko
Designer: Deborah Kaplan
Photography Editor: Christopher Bain
Photo Researcher: Ede Rothaus
Production Manager: Karen L. Greenberg

*Thanks to Richard Faber,
well known ocean liner memorabilia
collector and dealer.*

Typeset by Mar + x Myles Graphics, Inc.
Color separations by Universal Colour Scanning, Ltd.
Printed and bound in Hong Kong by Leefung-Asco Printers Ltd.

For Dick Faber

collector, connoisseur of ships, helpful friend

THE
FIRST
OCEAN
LINERS

AN OCEAN LINER IS MOST EASILY DEFINED AS A BIG OR MAJOR PASSENGER SHIP.

Certainly, the term conjures up an image, often romanticized, of a large vessel, usually with a

high bow and tall smokestacks (often two or more) "ripping" through active seas. Although

smaller passenger ships have every right to be called "liners," it is perhaps best—and in view of

the limitations of this generalized work—to think of the bigger ships as "ocean liners," and the

smaller ones as "passenger ships."

The first ocean liner (and certainly the first "superliner") was Germany's *Kaiser Wilhelm*

der Grosse, built in 1897. The *Kaiser* symbolized the flowering of late 19th-century maritime

technology. Those 10 or so decades before her had witnessed extraordinary progress—from

small, wood-hulled sailing ships to the earliest steamers, the paddle wheelers, the first iron ship

and then (noticeably growing in size, speed, and grandeur) to the first three- and four-stackers.

The power of the turn-of-the-century big Germans was perhaps best exemplified by their quartets of towering smokestacks. Very quickly, the travelling public equated the number of funnels with size, speed, and even safety. Consequently, the "four-stackers" were always the most sought-after ships. Their royal names also added to their favor, especially in the watchful eyes of Berlin ministers.

Passage times were cut continuously, and quite often, the extravagance and novelty of accommodation expanded. It was, however, primarily a British century of sea travel. That ever-growing empire, with its skilled sailors and shipbuilders, appeared to be the only country capable of running successful passenger ships.

Nevertheless, in that final decade, the latest contender for "world's largest" and "world's fastest" liner flew the German colors. The most serious maritime rivalry yet, a great technological race, had begun and would continue in the decades to follow, adding the French, the Italians, and finally the Americans themselves. But that first challenge was between two imperial giants: vast, rich, but seemingly too contented Victorian Britain and a young, surging, ever-expansive Germany. Actually, the new German record breaker came from an idea sparked some eight years earlier, in 1889, and from a British ship no less. It was during a summer-time fleet review at Spithead in England, attended by both the Prince of Wales (later Edward VII) and his nephew, William II, the Emperor of Germany,

The first great German four-stackers of the turn-of-the-century were actually more popular in the United States than in their homeland. During her first call, in the spring of 1903, a staggering 40,000 visitors toured the brand new Kaiser Wilhelm II. *These ships were especially well known within New York harbor. They were equally popular more locally, at their berths on the western shore of the Hudson, where they were fondly dubbed "the Hohenzollerns of Hoboken."*

that the maritime rivalry got its start. Impressed with the power of the British fleet, the German emperor determined to build his own navy, with the ultimate goal of building a colonial empire to match that of Britain.

It was the advent of the steamship decades before that made it all possible. In 1819, the little American-owned *Savannah,* a ship of only 151 feet (45m) in length and with a capacity for a mere 32 passengers, was fitted with a small steam engine that assisted both her sails and her

ingeniously removable paddle wheel. She crossed, in 24 days, from Savannah, Georgia to the Irish Coast. Although the steam engine was used for only 90 hours in all, it represented a new dimension, a new era—the age of steam! It would be, however, another 20 years before an equally small paddle wheeler, the *Sirius,* made an entire crossing under steam—for 17 days at eight knots. This was another turning point. Clearly, the days of the full sailing ships were numbered. Yet even aboard the *Sirius* and for some decades to come, sails were carried just in case. The major problem for these early steamers, however, was their difficulty in attracting passengers. Crew members and travelers alike, and perhaps more importantly, the general public, were unsure of these new ships. They were said to be "uncertain vessels," irregular, and—most image-damaging of all—they were said to be unsafe.

It was Britain's Cunard Steam-Ship Company Limited, then a brand-new firm based out of Liverpool, that reversed many of these prejudices. Samuel Cunard, the company founder, insisted that safety be placed above speed—whatever the cost. It was, he said, better to have safe and reliable steamers than speedy ones. Cunard's priority was to cut down the number of

Four-masted to resemble the great sailing ships and white-hulled to resemble a royal yacht, the *Kaiser Wilhelm II* (opposite page) was an exceptionally luxurious vessel. In the 1880s, she ran some of the very first deluxe cruises—voyages to what were then exotic destinations: the Mediterranean, Scandinavia, even the Arctic. The little *Savannah* (left) was a classic: the first steamer ever to cross the North Atlantic. She was especially honored in the late 1950s, when America's first nuclear-powered ship took her name. But unfortunately, the NS SAVANNAH did not become a groundbreaker as expected— very few nuclear vessels have followed in her wake.

days spent at sea rather than trying to outpace the other fast packets just for record's sake. The Cunard name soon became almost synonymous with reliability and punctuality, and the public's outlook on steam ships began to change.

In the decade between 1840 and 1850, Cunarders—as their ships were also called—set the pace and even captured the Blue Ribbon, the prized record for the best speed across the Atlantic. Their ships were then averaging a very impressive 12 knots and had cut the passage time between Liverpool and Halifax down to nine and a half days. The first Cunarder to establish a record was the aptly-named *Britannia,* a steam packet that was also fully rigged as a bark. Her wooden hull was 228 feet (68 m) in length (within a century, a successor in the same fleet, the *Queen Elizabeth,* would be more than four times this length). She and her fleetmates, then known as "teakettles," had not only fostered a more positive image of steam as transport, but also established British superiority on the Atlantic. In 1841, for example, Cunarders made 40 crossings—all of them safe and all of them under steam. And even if, by the 1850s, there were still as many as 150 sailing ships to every single steamer, the new age had arrived—steam was here to stay.

*F*og was a dreaded prospect for all seafarers, but especially for the liners. Collisions were frequent. In 1900, Cunard's Campania sliced in half a bark on the Irish sea. Eleven died. A year later, White Star's Oceanic rammed a coastal freighter off the English coast and seven lives were lost. In 1908, the American liner St. Paul collided with the British cruiser Gladiator. The warship sank, claiming 27 lives.

Comfort and luxury had, however, not yet arrived in Atlantic passenger ships. Charles Dickens, who crossed on Cunard's *Britannia* in 1842 bitterly complained, "The dining room is like a gigantic hearse with windows," and then regarding the cabins, "I felt like a giraffe being persuaded into a flowerpot." It was, despite British domination, an American who brought luxury to the North Atlantic. The steamers that belonged to Edward K. Collins through his Collins Line quickly became known as "the palaces of the Atlantic." His brand new quartet—the 2,800-ton (2,520 t) *Atlantic, Pacific, Arctic,* and *Baltic*—were fashioned after, of all things, the famed Mississippi riverboats. They featured Italian marble on board, stained glass windows, and even the wonder of an adjustable chair in the ship's barbershop. This luxury was coupled with attentive service and fine cuisine. Green turtle soup and goose in champagne sauce were among the Collins Line's dinner offerings. By 1852, these new Collins ships, the American-flag response "to the conquest of that man Cunard," seemed to be succeeding. But ship operations were a very precarious business. Evidently for Collins, the cost of such high luxury was too great. Even though in 1852 some 4,300 passengers traveled on Collins luxury ships compared to 2,900 in the more austere Cunarders, the glory was short-lived. Collins amassed losses in the same year of $1.7 million, a staggering amount for that time. By 1858, in just short of a decade since his firm was formed, the last of the Collins fleet went to the auction block. The Blue Ribbon record that had been set by a Collins ship, the *Baltic,* also faded. It passed to yet another Cunarder, the *Scotia.* The British, mostly in the name of the rather conservative Cunard Company, thereafter continued to dominate the transatlantic passenger trade. They held almost all Atlantic records, for speed as well as size, until the autumn of 1897, when that aforementioned German contender, the *Kaiser Wilhelm der Grosse,* first appeared.

The little *Britannia,* (opposite page) with her side-paddlewheels and her masts rigged for sails, arrives on her historic trip to Boston. She's the splendid forerunner to the Cunard fleet that, in 1990, celebrated 150 years of Atlantic service. Her reliability was her asset. Speed was also a great priority. Cunard's *Scotia,* (above) a Blue Ribbon champion of the late 1850s, was therefore guaranteed special popularity and high profitability.

She was the most extraordinary creation of her day—by far the biggest passenger ship yet to sail the seas. Even today, the *Great Eastern* is unique: the only ship ever to have 5 smokestacks and 6 masts! Note also in this view of the comparisons made to far smaller sailing ships. The splendid drawings (far right) by Scott Russell detail the ship's monstrous engines for her paddlewheels. The longitudinal drawing highlights her pencil-thin funnels and the overview reveals the expansive main deck space and the arrangement of her lifeboats, which include two large steam launches.

There are, however, a number of other passenger ships that plied the seas before 1897 that are worthy of at least a brief mention. By far the greatest hint of the ocean giants yet to come, particularly in the early years of the next century, was the 18,900-ton (17,010 t) *Great Eastern*. She was, at least in the eyes of her creator, a brilliant genius named Isambard Kingdom Brunel, the floating centerpiece of British brilliance, extravagance, and marvel. To others, perhaps more objective, she was a ship that was well ahead of her time. When she was launched, she was five times larger than any other existing vessel and the first and only passenger ship to have five stacks and six masts! A colossus in every way, she had not only a single screw propeller as

well as side paddle wheels, but also a full set of sails. The engine room alone had ten boilers that were fed by 100 furnaces!

The *Great Eastern* was actually designed for the long-haul run from England out to Australia, but this journey never came about and instead she was placed on the booming North Atlantic. Sadly, however, she was a folly, the big white elephant. She never earned any profit. Her 4,000 passenger berths went largely unfilled. She was too large for her time, her career was further darkened by several costly accidents, and in the process, she even bankrupted several firms. In the very end, she was reduced first to cable-laying duties and then was permanently moored as a floating "fun fair and carnival ship." In retrospect, however, the 689-foot (207 m) long *Great Eastern* fascinated many people. In her day, she was the genius ship of the future, and even if it would take another 40 or so years before her dimensions would be surpassed, she was a forerunner of the age of the "superliner."

By the 1890s, all of the big Atlantic passenger ship companies were doing well, and some were extremely successful. The prospects for the passenger ship business were very encourag-

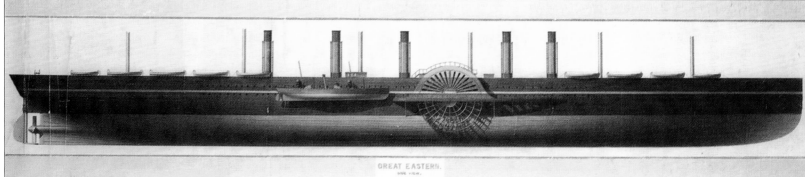

GREAT EASTERN.
SIDE VIEW.

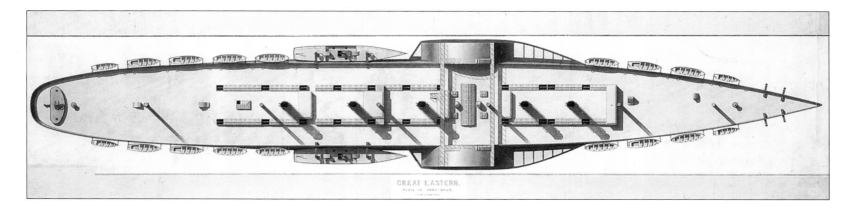

GREAT EASTERN.
PLAN OF SPAR DECK.

ing. Four out of every five passengers in first and second class were Americans, traveling on business or for pleasure (on those grand summer tours, among other sojourns) plus there was the steadily increasing, very profitable immigrant trade in third class and steerage. Yet these passengers, whether their fares were $500 for a lavish first-class suite (1890) or six dollars for a cramped berth in steerage, had their demands. Generally, they wanted bigger, faster, and safer ships. And so the shipping companies, from their marble-walled corporate offices in London and Liverpool, Bremen and Hamburg, and New York, responded by giving the traveling public bigger and better ships. In 1888–89, just as most of the canvas sails were finally disappearing and as steam became the sole source of power, four noted passenger ships appeared. Again, all of them flew the Union Jack. Each of them was 10,000 tons (9,000 t) and capable of as much as 20 knots. They were the Inman Line's *City of New York* and *City of Paris,* and the White Star Line's *Majestic* and *Teutonic.* The earlier pair, with their three funnels and elegant clipper-ship bows, would eventually pass into American ownership; the second two were the most serious rivals to the other mighty British shipper, Cunard.

Cunard itself finally responded, in 1893, with a splendid pair of ships—the largest and fastest yet on the Atlantic—the sisters *Campania* and *Lucania,* each 13,000 tons (11,700 t). Capable of an astounding 22 knots, they were "ships of wonder"—the first to have electric light throughout, revolving chairs in the restaurant, gilded pipes in the organ, and tiles from Persia.

It was, however, not a Cunarder that so impressed the German kaiser on that summer afternoon at Spithead, in 1889. It was a tour around White Star's *Teutonic,* a rival ship. Even the fierce British dreadnoughts did not overshadow that smart-looking passenger ship. Kaiser Wilhelm was charmed and intrigued by the high standard of her décor: the use of leather in the chairs and sofas, the intricately carved woodwork, the gilded accent pieces, and the extensive use of electric light. But he was absolutely fascinated by the general design of the ship and her then novel dual purpose. With special armor added to parts of her hull and with small guns scattered about her open, upper decks, she could also serve as a wartime armed merchant

cruiser. A passenger ship that might also be a warship: this is what thoroughly impressed the kaiser. He envisioned dual-purpose German liners, but bigger and faster still. Upon leaving the *Teutonic,* he was said to remark, "We must have some of these."

The Germans were planning to become a major sea power at that time, and what better way than with the marvels of their day: ocean liners. Furthermore, they wanted to prove their industrial and technological might, especially to the rest of the world, and thus planned to build such new ships not in masterful British shipyards, but in their home waters, using German shipbuilders. They would, of course, borrow skills and secrets as well as craftsmen from British yards and then, after mastering their methods, send their Belfast and Glasgow teachers packing. And so came the age of the *Kaiser Wilhelm der Grosse* and the first set of Teutonic record breakers. The Atlantic run would never be quite the same again.

The German presence on the North Atlantic was divided between two important firms, the Hamburg America Line and the North German Lloyd. Both had extensive fleets, passenger ships mostly of smaller and more moderate sizes that sailed not only to New York but also to the

Inman Line's *City of New York* was a classic liner for her time, the 1880s. The detailed spoons (far left) were commemorative pieces that have persisted to this day. One collector has over 2,000 different ones. Shipboard life (above), especially up until the turn-of-the-century and the advent of the larger, more secure steamers, was not always tranquil. Storms and gales, ferocious seas, and even blizzards were dreaded by passenger ship captains.

*W*hen they commissioned the Kaiser Wilhelm
der Grosse *in 1897, the Germans beamed with
pride. Not only did they design and own her, but
they built her as well. No longer were the big
British shipyards, in England, Scotland, and
Northern Ireland the master ocean liner builders.
Now there were skilled and serious competitors at
ports such as Bremen and Hamburg,
Stettin and Geestmunde.*

West Indies and South America, to the Far East, and to Australia. Neither firm seemed interested in big liners or transatlantic records until the 1890s. At that time, their plans changed, prompted mostly by the Kaiser himself, but also by the steadily increasing numbers of passengers, and the pure profit potential of it all. There was even a third reason: existing German passenger tonnage was aging and needed to be replaced—naturally, they should produce bigger, faster, and grander ships than their nearest rivals, the British.

Of course, there was a rivalry between the two German firms as well, and so, once the Kaiser's wishes were known, both companies planned larger passenger ships. Berlin insisted that these ships be bigger and, if possible, faster than any existing British vessels. The Lloyd operation seemed the keenest at first. They went to the Vulcan Shipyards of Stettin and stated, "Build us the fastest passenger ship in the world and we'll buy it; give us anything less, and you can keep it." The design team at the Vulcan works responded, creating a long, slender ship fitted with the most powerful machinery yet to go to sea and, as if full proof of her abilities, she was capped by no less than four tall funnels, the first ship ever to have that number.

To the Kaiser himself, this ship was a dream boat, something of a personal *wunder* ship. He personally attended the launching, held in May of 1897. The ship was named for his grandfather, William I, the first emperor of Germany. Even incomplete, while lying at her berth, she looked strong and powerful, even lean. Adding to the buoyant enthusiasm, she was to be the first of a projected quartet—the number of boats then needed to offer a weekly sailing from each side of the Atlantic.

The new liner's maiden voyage would certainly be one of the most dramatic of all. German might would be visible for all to see. On board, the rigging was strung between two tall masts, her funnels painted the Lloyd's trademark mustard yellow, and the interior decoration completed. There were carved wood panels and crystal lamps, velvet sofas and brocade drapes, columned lounges and marbled fireplaces, and stained glass heretofore seen only in churches. The decorative statement was designed to overwhelm (an approach that would persist for decades). It was to create an indelible impression. It was to be palatial, luxurious, a floating fantasy world. The new *Kaiser* would take as many as 558 passengers in sumptuous first

Proud and tall and, above all, sturdy-looking, the *Kaiser Wilhelm der Grosse* was the world's largest liner—a prized and envied distinction—when she was completed in 1897. Her steel hull was trim and lean; the bulkier, ornate stylings of early paddlewheelers was past. This German began a new age of passenger shipping: the age of the super-liners, the Atlantic greyhounds. Design and dimensions of future tonnage could only expand.

17

The British responded to the *Kaiser Wilhelm der Grosse* in 1899 with the *Oceanic* (below), but the Germans had an even bigger liner, the *Kronprinz Wilhelm*, by 1901. Early passenger photos are increasingly rare. One of the very best collections still kept might be the Hamburg America Line's archives at Hamburg. Priceless photos and negatives are kept in meticulous order—even the scenes of passengers are still grouped by class.

class (where special suites could cost as much as $2,000 per person for the week-long passage), 338 passengers in slightly less spacious, perhaps slightly less comfortable second class and, most profitable of all to her owners, 1,074 passengers in steerage (about $10 a head).

The *Kaiser Wilhelm der Grosse* swept the North Atlantic in the autumn of 1897. She made the run to New York in a very impressive five days and 20 hours, at an average speed of 22.35 knots. The Blue Ribbon was in German hands and would remain with them for the next 10 years. The British, and specifically that giant in the Atlantic passenger industry, the Cunard Line, were startled, even furious. Yet their response came not until two years later, in 1899, when White Star's *Oceanic* at 17,200 tons (15,480 t) outsized the *Kaiser*, which weighed "only" 14,300 tons (12,870 t), to become the "world's largest." These statistically distinctive

ships, whether for speed or dimensions, were always extremely popular. They always had the slight competitive edge and were therefore almost assured full profitability.

The Hamburg America Line, the nearest rival to the Lloyd and their new flagship, were

envious as well. Immediately, they planned a record breaker of their own, a ship larger still, at

over 16,000 tons (14,400 t). Maritime rivalries were not limited simply to nations, but existed as

well between shipowners, even those flying the same national flag. In 1900, this new ship, the

Deutschland, easily took the Ribbon. She too was a four-stacker, grand and perhaps over-

gilded, and very popular, at least in the beginning. She developed, however, problems that

were worrisome to the owners of fast liners. The *Deutschland* had great speed, but it was at the

passengers' expense. There were vibrations, rattling, and excessive noises from her soaring

quadruple expansion engines. Earlier, the White Star Line had claimed that they were not inter-

ested in high speed if it risked passenger comfort. Now, the Hamburg America Line began to

feel the same way. Hereafter, both of these major firms would emphasize comfort and luxury

over record speed. While the sleek *Deutschland* managed to hold the Ribbon for six years,

until 1906, the effort was costly. She was not considered a very successful ship.

The North German Lloyd soon built three other giants: the *Kronprinz Wilhelm* in 1901, the *Kaiser Wilhelm II* in 1903, and finally the *Kronprinzessin Cecilie* in 1906. In those briskly competitive times, the last pair, at over 19,000 tons (17,000 t) were also noted as the "world's largest." But ambitious plans sometimes go astray, even plans for methodically designed German ocean liners. Both ships were intended not only to be large, but also to be speed record breakers, but the estimates for their reserve power were somewhat inflated. The *Kaiser Wilhelm II* succeeded only briefly, for a short time in 1906–07; the *Kronprinzessin Cecilie* never managed a record run at all.

The four Lloyd "greyhounds," as they were called, ran a precision service on the Atlantic: weekly sailings between New York (the actual terminal was across the Hudson, in Hoboken) and then across to Cherbourg, Southampton, and Bremerhaven. They were extremely successful and very popular. It was claimed that "the finest hotels in the world do not boast of more gorgeous splendor." With each successive new ship, there seemed to be more luxury, more marble, certainly more gilt. The Lloyd also established one of the earliest passenger marketing patterns. Very quickly, the four mighty funnels onboard each were equated with size, speed, luxury and, perhaps above all else and especially to those often worried souls in lower-deck steerage, safety. Everyone wanted to sail in ships with several funnels and so, while the three-stackers were very popular, the four-stackers were blockbusters.

Sadly, these big Germans barely survived the First World War. Ironically, the very country that had created them—and so many other, smaller passenger ships—was now responsible for their demise. The *Kaiser Wilhelm der Grosse* was sunk off West Africa while serving as an armed merchant cruiser in the first grey days of battle in August, 1914. The troublesome *Deutschland,* having been remade into a special cruise ship called the *Victoria Luise,* sailed for a short time as the downgraded migrant ship *Hansa.* The last three liners fell into American hands during the war years and later served as Allied troop transports, carrying the infamous doughboys to fight German armies in the trenches of western Europe. Afterward, deteriorated and exhausted, the former *Kronprinz Wilhelm* was scrapped, and the ex-*Kaiser Wilhelm II* and the ex-*Kronprinzessin Cecilie* were sent to the backwaters of the Chesapeake, where various plans to revive them never came to pass. This final pair went off the junkheaps in 1940.

It has always been rather amazing that America did not invest heavily in transatlantic passenger shipping. At best, the efforts of firms such as the American Line tended to be rather moderate and have limited success. Perhaps American interests looked westward, to the growing nation, rather than eastward, back to a European heritage. Years later, when the *Leviathan* was proclaimed the largest liner ever to fly the Stars & Stripes, it remains rather ironic that she was in fact not an American-built ship, but instead one inherited as a prize of the First World War.

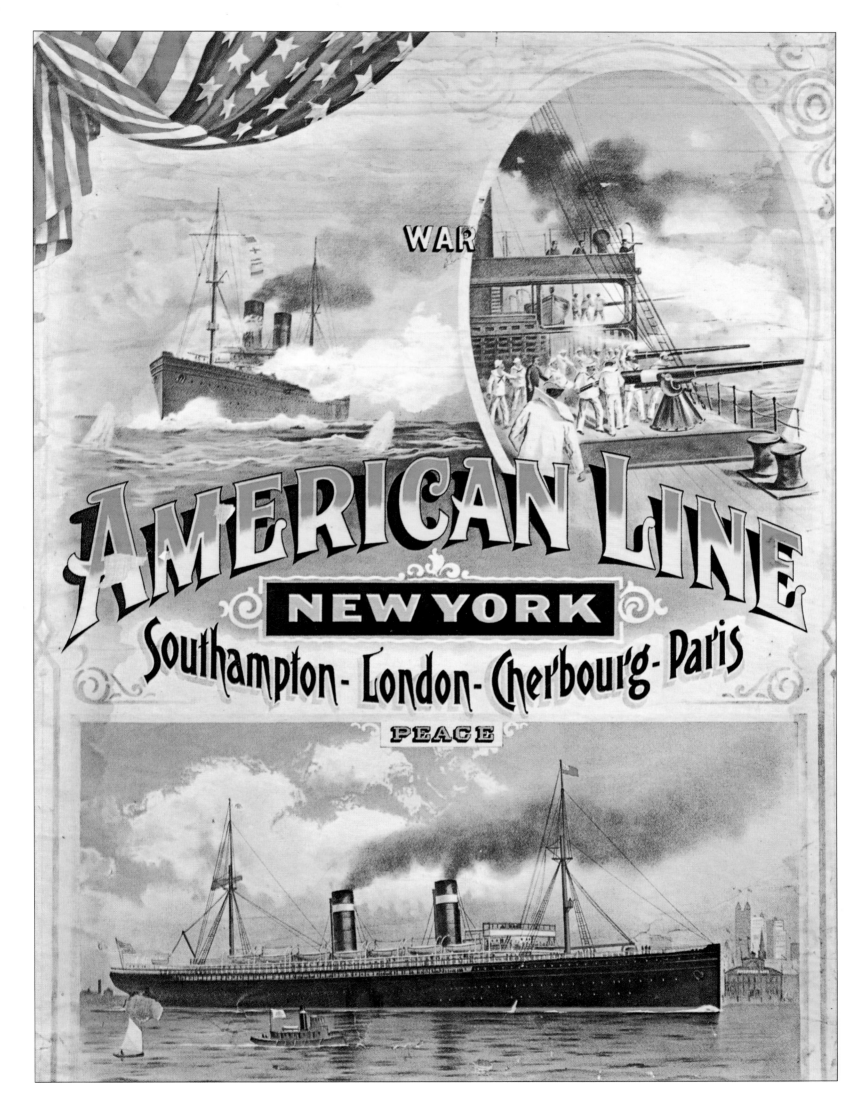

THE FLOATING PALACES

THE CREATION OF THOSE FOUR BIG GERMAN LINERS, BEGINNING WITH THE SPEEDY

Kaiser Wilhelm der Grosse, was a blunt awakening, a great shock in fact, to the British and their

long supremacy on the North Atlantic. Something had to be done to regain their status. The

transoceanic trade continued to boom and to expand—there were more travelers, mostly

Americans, in first and second class, and millions going westbound in third class and steerage.

Bigger ships were surely in the wind and would be guaranteed highly profitable lives.

In particular, the British wanted those prized distinctions for "world's fastest" and

"world's largest" back in their hands, safely entrusted to liners flying the Red Ensign. They

would have to wait for a full decade for the Blue Ribbon trophy for speed, however. The *Kaiser*

Wilhelm der Grosse had it for three years from 1897, before the honors went to the *Deutsch-*

land, which remained unchallenged for nearly six years, until 1906. One final German ship,

the *Kaiser Wilhelm II,* then had it for a short spell in 1906–07. It was not until then that the

British made their successful bid.

The glamor of the great ocean liners was dazzling. The French Line in particular became synonomous with high luxury. One example was a grand staircase in the three-deck high main restaurant aboard.

The record for "world's largest" was just as fierce a battle between the British and the Germans, especially as it was symbolic of the nations' technological advances, namely the

The Aquitania of 1914 was the last of the North Atlantic's four-stackers. Only two more were built, the sisters Arundel Castle and Windsor Castle of 1920–22, but for England-to-South Africa trades. All except the Aquitania were gone by the Second World War; she was the last four-funneler, and was finally scrapped in 1950.

expansive strides then being made in the art of shipbuilding. The 14,300-ton (12,870 t) *Kaiser Wilhelm der Grosse* was the largest by 1897, but was eclipsed two years later by the 17,200-ton (15,480 t) *Oceanic* of Britain's White Star Line. Within two years, White Star broke its own record with the first ships to exceed 20,000 tons (18,000 t), the sisters *Celtic* (1901) and *Cedric* (1903). It is also interesting to note that, although three and four funnels were preferred on the Atlantic run, White Star directors and designers were more conservative when creating this new pair of liners. These ships were given four masts, but only two funnels, supposedly with the effect of reminding prospective passengers of those great and revered sailing ships of the previous century. The idea worked well and was used in the next White Star team, the 23,800-ton (21,420 t) *Adriatic* and *Baltic* of 1904 and 1906. Once again, the British had built the world's largest liners. In 1906, Germany briefly retaliated with the 24,500-ton (22,050 t) *Kaiserin Auguste Victoria*. Yet even bigger liners were just around the corner.

The new liners were unabashedly luxurious as well. While there were salons of carved wood in the *Celtic* and marble bathtubs in the first-class suites on the *Adriatic,* the *Kaiserin Auguste Victoria* introduced the novelty of the grill room to her first-class travelers. It was an amenity separate from the usual dining room and even required a special admittance fee. The

offerings were epicurean: more turtle soups, a tank of fresh lobsters, and even specialties like

grilled oxen and fillet of zander. Passengers could dine at any hour and enjoyed white-gloved,

heel-clicking service. Other shipboard restaurants grew and became more ornate. Lounges

were extended to the full width of the ship. The first elevators appeared. Gymnasiums and

indoor "swimming baths," as they were called, also went aboard. And, in that constant quest to

have at least most of the first-class passengers forget that they were at sea aboard a rolling ship,

lush winter gardens with exotic foliage, plants, and even rattan furniture were installed. The

ship began to resemble a grand garden room right in the middle of the Atlantic Ocean.

Of course, the immigrants remained the most lucrative and therefore, in ways, the most

sought-after passengers. Even if their fares were as little as ten dollars each, they received so

little in the way of shipboard catering, accommodation, and actual space that this amount,

multiplied by as much as three thousand, made considerable profits for home office treasuries.

The general figures were mind-boggling. Between 1900 and 1914, over twelve million people

The first decades of the twentieth century were largely experimental. Britain's *Cedric* of 1903 (opposite page), for example, represented conservatism: a sensible, almost simple look that even used the four tall masts reminiscent of the sailing ship era. By comparison, two decades or so later (above), the Italians experimented with vast, uncluttered lido decks, tiled pools, open-air bars, and even real sand.

In the first decade of the twentieth century, immigrants were arriving at New York at the rate of 12,000 a day. The ships would anchor in the Lower Bay, off the Quarantine Station, and all third class and steerage passengers would be disembarked into ferries and other small steamers and then sent to Ellis Island.

crossed the Atlantic in third class and steerage. In 1907 alone, there were over seven million such travelers. By 1914, one-third of America's population was foreign-born.

The immigrants lived in small, poorly ventilated, often claustrophobically cramped quarters, mostly in the bowels of the passenger ships. The living and dining spaces were often one and the same. First-class passengers sometimes traveled down to the steerage quarters, leaving the potted palm luxury of their upper deck quarters, for a look during a crossing . A reverse trip was unthinkable. In later years, immigrant women—usually desperate to earn extra money for their new lives in America—took in laundry during their voyages, which usually came from the first-class passengers.

By the turn of the century, however, steerage had actually improved somewhat. Medical facilities were introduced. Some immigrant women actually tried to time their last days of pregnancy with a crossing so that the babies could be delivered in the steerage infirmary. While many immigrants had to travel with their own eating utensils as well as bedding, the North German Lloyd was novel in lending enameled tableware to steerage passengers for the duration of their voyage. In another instance, during a particularly fierce rate war, the same German shipper even gave a blanket to each immigrant passenger as a memento. Many foreign steamship lines began to set up their own medical facilities, usually at dockside, for the inspection of outbound passengers long before many of them were subjected to those feared, often questionable examinations on Ellis Island. Other steamship owners developed feeder systems that often included small passenger steamers that delivered immigrants from neighboring countries to home ports. Most companies also began to provide some form of bedding, often straw mattresses, and the French Line went so far, in 1906, to offer not only portholes in steerage, but even electric light. The Hamburg America Line was perhaps the most elaborate and thoughtful. They created a complete immigrant village, fully equipped with laundry, fumiga-

Steerage quarters, such as these aboard the giant German *Imperator,* were often more austere. Immigrants sometimes had to travel with their own eating utensils and even their own bedding.

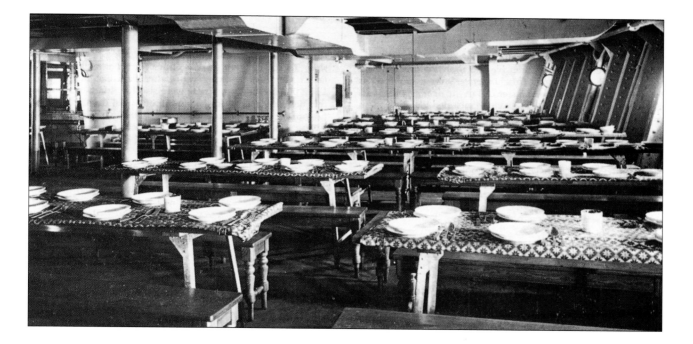

tion center, and even an entertaining brass band, before feeding passengers into westbound liners. By 1913–14, in that final heyday of unrestricted migration to the New World, the biggest liners, such as Hamburg America's *Vaterland,* were even fitted with steerage dining halls with uniformed stewards.

The liner business had become big business. In 1902, in another serious blow to the British, American tycoon J. P. Morgan formed the International Mercantile Marine and bought no less than six British passenger ship firms, including the well-known Red Star, Dominion, and Leyland lines. But the absolute jewel in this acquisition was the entire capital stock of the mighty White Star Company, surely one of the biggest and most illustrious firms in the passen-

Cunard's *Mauretania*, seen here at Southampton while undergoing her annual maintenance, was certainly one of the most illustrious liners of all time. She held the prized Blue Ribbon for twenty-two years, longer than any other liner.

ger business. White Star cost Morgan an extraordinary $25 million—all of it in gold. The British government was deeply shaken, shocked, and outraged. First, the Germans created bigger and faster liners, and now White Star was American-owned (it would continue, however, to be British in nature, use British crews, fly the Red Ensign, and keep its corporate seat in London). Again, something had to be done, and now more urgently than ever. Morgan was, in fact, on a buying spree. After a failed attempt to acquire a German line, he set his sights on Cunard. The British government wouldn't hear of it. London ministers offered Cunard's Liverpool directors a very enticing, quite irresistible alternative: a lavish loan of £2.6 million to build two very large, very fast express liners (that would have to surpass those of the Germans) and then a £150,000 annual operating subsidy as well. In return, Cunard had to agree to remain British for at least 20 years. Naturally, they accepted the offer, and the orders were given for a pair of British superships, the legendary *Mauretania* and the immortal *Lusitania*.

These new ships would also benefit from the results of a recent, rather bold experiment.

CUNARD

FASTEST OCEAN SERVICE IN THE WORLD

SOUTHAMPTON, CHERBOURG AND NEW YORK

R.M.S. "MAURETANIA"   R.M.S. "BERENGARIA"   R.M.S. "AQUITANIA"

In 1905, Cunard ran a noteworthy test with two brand new, 19,500-ton (17,550 t) sister ships, the *Carmania* and *Caronia*. The *Carmania* was completed with new steam turbine engines, the latest advance in the age of ship propulsion; her sister had the standard steam quadruple expansion type. The *Carmania* proved to be not only faster, but both more efficient and economical. The successful new steam turbine system would allow for faster liners, a new Atlantic team of record breakers. Each of the ships would be fitted with four giant turbines, so powerful that they were capable of generating 75 percent more power than an equivalent liner using the old reciprocating method. Assuredly, they would be far faster than those four-funnel German ships.

As was their tradition, Cunard gave their superliners names of Roman provinces— *Mauretania* for Morocco, *Lusitania* for Portugal. The former was built at Newcastle, while the latter came from one of the world's busiest shipbuilding centers, Scotland's River Clyde. They were also the largest ships of their day: nearly 32,000 tons (28,800 t) each (the first ever to surpass the 30,000-ton mark), just short of 800 feet (240 m) in length and eight decks in height. There were 25 boilers and 192 furnaces. Seventy-two trainloads of coal were needed to fill their bunkers—they consumed 1,000 tons of coal a day. They were the first liners to make the

Atlantic passage in under five days. The *Mauretania* proved to be slightly faster, her best record being four days, 19 hours. She remained unchallenged, much to the delight and pride of the British, for 22 years, until 1929. While there were certainly increasingly larger liners to come in the immediate years ahead, none of them had the reserve power to outpace the speedy *Mauretania*. Her record was finally taken by a new German ship, the *Bremen,* in the summer of 1929. The old Cunarder actually made one last attempt, and some furniture even went into the furnaces to muster extra speed, in a valiant but unsuccessful try.

Naturally, the *Mauretania* and *Lusitania* were beautifully decorated, although perhaps more conservative, even muted, when compared to those heavy, wooded, gilded German liners. Like many British liners to follow, and particularly the Cunarders, the overall tone was solid and reliable, not pretentious or extravagant. The decorative details were enticing just the same: public rooms in Italian and French Renaissance styles, restaurants in straw-colored oak capped by glass domes. Stateroom styles varied: Adam, Sheraton, Chippendale. The smoking room had a wagon-headed roof, special details copied from Italian villas, and the best wood veneers from British as well as French forests. Even the bathroom fittings were unique, made of white metal and in first class, they were silver-plated.

Everyone—the Germans, other British shippers (particularly the White Star Line) and even the French—were fascinated by these Cunard champions. Certainly, they heralded a new era in propulsion—the steam turbine was soon built into almost all ships. But in the continuing race for the largest, fastest, and finest, drawing boards were soon cleared only to take on projects (and schemes) for bigger liners still. White Star planned a trio, the number then needed for

When being designed, the two new express Cunarders, the *Mauretania* and *Lusitania* of 1907, might have had just three funnels each. But since they were intended to surpass the quartet of German four-stackers, the new British ships had to have at least an equal number of funnels. Almost every detail and element of design was inspired at least in part by this keen competition.

The Mauretania and the Lusitania were decoratively not as "heavy" as the earlier big Germans. Overall, the styles of the big Cunarders varied, perhaps giving their onboard guests a welcome sense of change. It was also an era when costs were less of a serious consideration. For example, 300 wood-carvers were imported from Palestine just to complete one lounge on the Mauretania.

a weekly relay between Southampton and New York; Cunard planned a third liner to join their new sisters and fill out their weekly timetable; the French would finally proceed with their first major liner; and the Germans, namely the Hamburg America Line, had the most startlingly ambitious plans of all for building a trio of successively larger superliners, the most colossal ever and the first to exceed 50,000 tons (45,000 t).

The respective governments financially endorsed and enthusiastically encouraged these big liner projects. These ships enhanced national goodwill and image. They were technological as well as decorative statements, the ideal floating ambassadors, particularly to the Americans. Again, and perhaps more than in the recent past, there was that desire to overwhelm, to produce something close to an exclusive floating world of grandeur and luxury. Secondly, governments saw the ships as valuable assets in times of war: they could be easily converted to powerful armed merchant cruisers, hospital ships or better still, high-capacity troop transports. Travelers themselves, particularly in first and second class, were delighted with the decorative styles, the novelties, the extreme spaciousness. Steerage voyagers favored them as well, feeling that these superships offered a safe, smooth trip across the often ferocious Atlantic.

The superliners were the marvels of their time, the "largest moving objects made by man." In this comparison, the 882-foot long *Olympic* is compared to the world's tallest structures in 1912: the City Hall at Philadelphia, the Washington Monument, the Metropolitan Life and Woolworth buildings (left); and Cologne Cathedral, the Pyramids, and St. Peter's (right).

WHITE STAR LINE R.M.S "OLYMPIC"
COMPARED WITH VARIOUS FAMOUS BUILDINGS.

The new White Star trio was planned as the "most splendid" ships on the transatlantic run. The first, the *Olympic,* the next contender in the world's largest sweepstakes, was launched in October, 1910 and was ready for service the following May. Her accommodations were arranged in rather prescribed fashion for the times: 1,054 passengers in ornate first class, 510 passengers in somewhat less spacious second class, and 1,020 passengers in third class. Her interiors were worthy of considerable attention. The first-class main lounge, for example, was copied from the palace at Versailles. The palm court had trellises of ivy and climbing green plants, and was intended to remind passengers of shore, if only mentally. The Turkish baths were Arabian in theme and included splendid bronze lamps and a marble drinking fountain. There were squash courts and the first "swimming bath" ever to go to sea. The staterooms were decorated in 11 different styles, from Italian Renaissance to old Dutch. Even the beds were noteworthy: they were said to be the widest afloat.

Furnishings and other objets d'art often lived on, passing from one liner to another. The chairs, for example, from the Aquitania's *Louis XVI restaurant were placed in storage after 1950. In 1956, after some refinishing and reupholstering, they reappeared in the first-class restaurant aboard the brand new Cunarder* Carinthia. *That ship was retired from Cunard service in 1968 and thereafter the whereabouts of those long-lived chairs became a mystery. Another part of the* Aquitania, *her magnificent carpets, did not go back aboard after World War II, but instead went to the* Britannic *and stayed with her until her retirement in 1960.*

In May, 1911, as the *Olympic* left her builder's berth at Belfast, the next White Star supership took her place at the outfitting dock. She was the immortal *Titanic.* Worried that this second liner would be overshadowed by her elder sister and just to give her an added cachet, her owners decided to dub her as the "world's safest ship," indeed, an unsinkable ship. To support this improbable distinction, she had far fewer lifeboats than she actually needed. In April, 1912, she departed on the most famous, most documented, and most disastrous maiden voyage ever. Rammed by an iceberg in the Western Atlantic, she sank. An estimated 1,522 people perished; a little less than a third, 705 passengers in all, were saved. More about the *Titanic's* devastating demise, the first catastrophe to befall the new generation of superliners, is included in Chapter Four, Disasters: The Lost Liners.

Ironically, the third of the White Star big liners never reached New York either. Larger still, at 48,100 tons (43,290 t), this ship was to be called *Gigantic.* She was renamed *Britannic,* however, which was considered a wiser choice following the tragic loss of her earlier fleetmate, and was due in 1915. Unfortunately, by then, the First World War had begun and the liner was sent

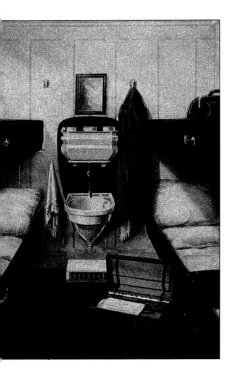

Artists certainly embellished the actual statistics of early ocean liners. They were made to appear longer, taller, more powerful—all with the aim of luring more passengers, particularly those in lower-deck steerage. Note the size of the third-class cabin and the innovative amenity of a washing sink.

directly into military service, as a hospital ship serving the Mediterranean campaigns. Sadly, in November, 1916, she was mined in the Aegean. The *Britannic* was only a year old.

Cunard's third superliner came from the illustrious John Brown shipyards on the Clyde. She was named *Aquitania*, this time for the Roman province that is now the south of France.

The decorative splendors of the liners had two important purposes: to attract passengers, especially the first class set, and to make a statement, the ships being the floating representatives of their nations. Certainly, the *Aquitania* was one of the very best—aptly called the "ship beautiful." Here is that ship's spectacular Palladian Lounge.

Again capped by four towering funnels, each painted in Cunard's black and distinctive orange-red, almost from the start she was praised as one of the most beautiful liners of all time. This included not only her smoothly raked profile, but her vast interiors, where there seemed to be a room of every style and period. There was a Palladian lounge, a Caroline smoking room, and a Louis XVI restaurant. The grill room was Jacobean, the lower-deck pool Egyptian. The *Aquitania* was also the most enduring of the early "floating palaces." She survived two world wars and even returned to the Atlantic run in the late forties, the last four-stacker of all, before going to the breakers located not far from where she was born 36 years earlier.

In April, 1909, the keel was laid for the new flagship of the French merchant marine. The new vessel was to be more than twice the size of any previous French liner. It had been intended to call this vessel *La Picardie,* but by the time of launching, in September, 1910, the name *France* was selected—and seemed more appropriate. Considerable attention was centered on this ship, even if the British and the Germans were either building or busily planning larger ones, for her decoration promised to make her one of the most stunning liners on the North Atlantic.

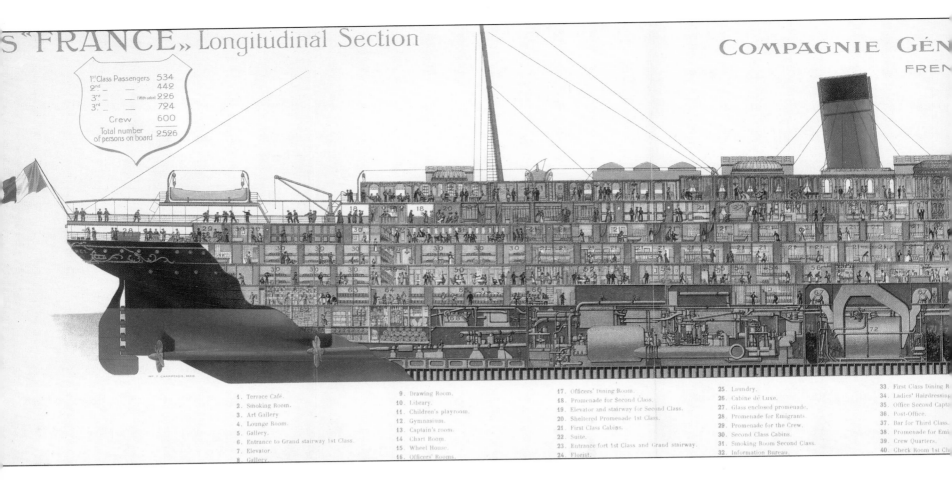

S "FRANCE" Longitudinal Section

COMPAGNIE GÉN

FREN

1st Class Passengers 534
2nd — — 442
3rd — (With cabin) 226
3rd — — 724
Crew 600
Total number
of persons on board 2526

1. Terrace Café.	9. Drawing Room.	17. Officers' Dining Room.	25. Laundry.	33. First Class Dining R
2. Smoking Room.	10. Library.	18. Promenade for Second Class.	26. Cabine de Luxe.	34. Ladies' Hairdressing
3. Art Gallery	11. Children's playroom.	19. Elevator and stairway for Second Class.	27. Glass enclosed promenade.	35. Office Second Capta
4. Lounge Room.	12. Gymnasium.	20. Sheltered Promenade 1st Class.	28. Promenade for Emigrants.	36. Post-Office.
5. Gallery.	13. Captain's room.	21. First Class Cabins.	29. Promenade for the Crew.	37. Bar for Third Class
6. Entrance to Grand stairway 1st Class.	14. Chart Room.	22. Suite.	30. Second Class Cabins.	38. Promenade for Emi
7. Elevator.	15. Wheel House.	23. Entrance fort 1st Class and Grand stairway.	31. Smoking Room Second Class.	39. Crew Quarters.
8. Gallery.	16. Officers' Rooms.	24. Florist.	32. Information Bureau.	40. Check Room 1st Cla

Just after the *Titanic* went to the bottom, the new *France* set off, on April 20, 1912, from her homeport of Le Havre on her gala maiden trip to New York. She settled in on the ocean circuit very quickly and very successfully. Her appearance was highlighted not only by her superb décor, but by her magnificent cuisine (she began each crossing, for example, with 18 barrels of pâté). Her first class was soon a favorite of the transatlantic social set, those million-aires and titled aristocrats who usually made more than one annual commute. The 23,600-ton (21,240 t) *France* led to a superb French Line quartet, beginning with the splendid 34,500-ton (31,050 t) *Paris* of 1921.

It was the Germans, however, who seemed to pull out all the stops in those last high-spirited, almost carefree days just before the start of the Great War. The Hamburg America Line, the largest shipping company on earth with well over 400 vessels (in 1914), was not to be outdone, outsized, and certainly not outclassed by "those British across the Channel," namely Cunard and White Star, and so planned three progressively larger liners, the largest ever to go to sea. And so, in June, 1910, the keel plates were laid down for what was aptly called "the colos-

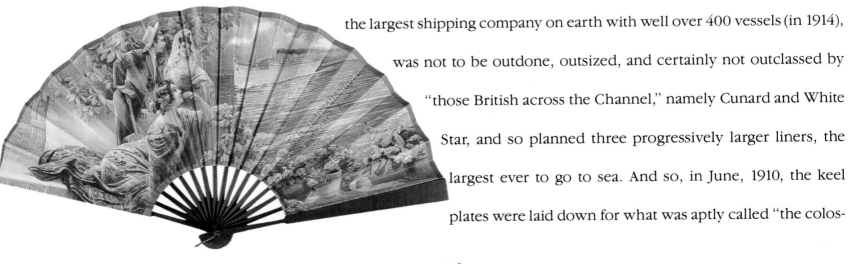

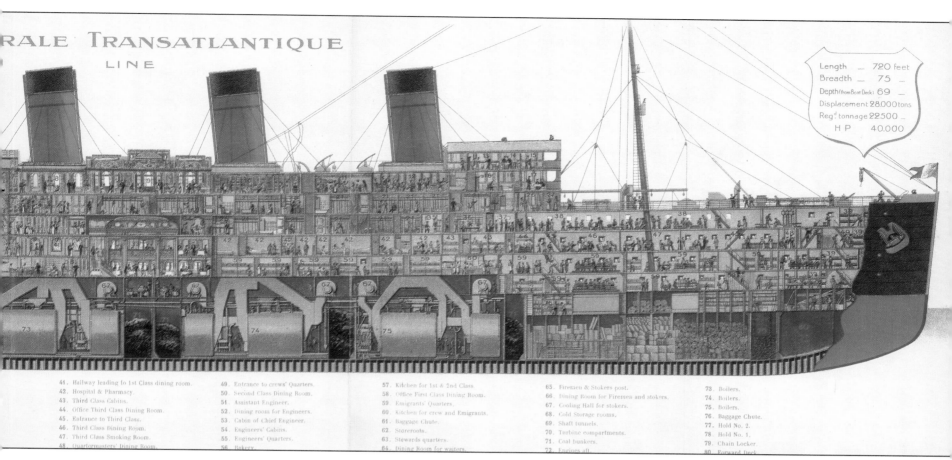

RALE TRANSATLANTIQUE
LINE

Length — 720 feet
Breadth — 75 —
Depth (from Boat Deck) 69 —
Displacement 28,000 tons
Reg.d tonnage 22,500
H P 40,000

41. Railway leading to 1st Class dining room.	49. Entrance to crews' Quarters.	57. Kitchen for 1st & 2nd Class.	65. Firemen & Stokers post.	73. Boilers.
42. Hospital & Pharmacy.	50. Second Class Dining Room.	58. Office First Class Dining Room.	66. Dining Room for Firemen and stokers.	74. Boilers.
43. Third Class Cabins.	51. Assistant Engineer.	59. Emigrants' Quarters.	67. Cooling Hall for stokers.	75. Boilers.
44. Office Third Class Dining Room.	52. Dining room for Engineers.	60. Kitchen for crew and Emigrants.	68. Cold Storage rooms.	76. Baggage Chute.
45. Entrance to Third Class.	53. Cabin of Chief Engineer.	61. Baggage Chute.	69. Shaft tunnels.	77. Hold No. 2.
46. Third Class Dining Room.	54. Engineers' Cabins.	62. Storeroom.	70. Turbine compartments.	78. Hold No. 1.
47. Third Class Smoking Room.	55. Engineers' Quarters.	63. Stewards quarters.	71. Coal bunkers.	79. Chain Locker.
48. Quartermasters' Dining Room.	56. Bakery.	64. Dining Room for waiters.	72. Engines aft.	80. Forward Deck.

sus" of the Atlantic. This new liner was to be called *Europa,* but in consideration of the kaiser's keen personal interest in the project, *Imperator* became the more fitting name.

The new superliner's statistics were even more mind-boggling for the time: 83 lifeboats in addition to a pair of special motor launches, a rudder weighing 90 tons, a quartet of four-bladed propellers that could make 185 revolutions per minute, and bunkers for 8,500 tons of coal. Her lavish quarters included a first-class lounge that could seat 700 passengers at once and a room capped by a glass dome. There was a Pompeiian bath, a twin to the one installed at London's Royal Automobile Club, as well as a very extensive gymnasium (the German liners seemed to have a predilection for electrical slimming devices). Her overall accommodations were also among the very largest yet to put to sea: 4,594 passengers in all—908 in first class, 972 in second class, 942 in third class, and 1,772 in steerage. Her staff numbered 1,180.

The 52,100-ton (46,890t) *Imperator* set off from Hamburg (the nearby port of Cuxhaven was actually used) for New York in June, 1913. Her passengers were especially reassured that she carried a large searchlight, presumably to spot nighttime icebergs and so diminish the possibilities of suffering a fate similar to that of the *Titanic.* The new imperial German flagship received great attention and acclaim, but her inaugural season was marked by one very serious

The longitudinal cross-sections of the great liners were particularly favored commemorative items. The detail, seemingly with every cabin, stairwell and engine room boiler, exemplified the "floating city" qualities of the biggest ships. Today, items like the exquisite commemorative fan below are prized, highly valued pieces of maritime memorabilia.

blemish, a problem grave enough to ruin her reputation and therefore her economic success: she was top-heavy. She always had a list. Transatlantic travelers, especially the privileged passengers in first class, tended to gossip about the great ships, avidly discussing their styles and crews, and also noting their flaws. Hamburg America was rightfully worried and so, in the

ship's first annual overhaul, the *Imperator*'s monstrous three funnels (the third, in fact, was a dummy, like many others, added more for effect than for any useful purpose) were cut down by nine feet so as to improve the overall balance. Internally, many of the marble fittings and heavy furniture were removed, and tons of cement were poured along the bottom as well. Even a bronzed decorative eagle, fitted to the bow in Hamburg America's final attempt to surpass the length of Cunard's 901-ft (270 m) long *Aquitania,* was not replaced after being lost in a violent storm. These renovations made the 919-ft (276 m) *Imperator* more stable and her reputation was saved.

If the *Imperator* was the biggest luxury liner yet, her sister, the *Vaterland,* would be bigger still at 54,000 tons (48,780 t). She was placed in service in May, 1914, only months away from the outbreak of war. In one of the greatest miscalculations by the Germans, she was left at her Hoboken berth in New York harbor as the conflict escalated. Plans for further German wonder ships also went astray. In the end, these liners saw very brief service under the home flag: the *Imperator* had only two seasons on the Atlantic, the *Vaterland* just a few months, and the third, the *Bismarck,* never appeared at all.

The *Vaterland,* despite her short reign on the Atlantic, was also highly praised and

Among the luxurious shops aboard the *Imperator* was a flower shop. The winged figure (above) was the emblem of the Hamburg America Line.

admired. She had a large winter garden, a grill room, elaborate lounges, a magnificent smoking room, an entire row of shops, a full bank, a travel bureau, and (reflecting Germany's continuing obsession with rigorous exercises and cold showers) an even more elaborate gymnasium and another large indoor pool. Her cabin accommodations included two lavish imperial suites. Structurally, she had extra-strengthened hull plates and the best fire prevention system afloat.

The third German giant, the *Bismarck,* launched in June, 1914, would have come into Atlantic service the following year. Instead, with the war underway, this 56,500-ton (50,850 t) ship sat out those hideous years as a rusting, darkened shell. The Kaiser and the entire imperial family had planned to take the mighty liner on an around-the-world victory cruise. Instead, by 1918–1919, the Germans had lost the war, the Kaiser was in exile, and the unfinished *Bismarck* was surrendered to the Allies.

Of the giants mentioned in this chapter, both the *Lusitania* and the *Britannic* were war losses—in fact, those two ships are still lingering in their underwater graves. The venerable

Hamburg-America Line's motto was *"Mein Feld ist die Welt"*—the world is my scope. Their ships traded to almost every corner of the globe, and many of them were among the finest at sea. They included every conceivable amenity, including a first-class onboard flower ship. In 1913, they owned the biggest liner yet built, the 52,100-ton *Imperator,* shown departing from her Hoboken berth.

Mauretania, perhaps the most legendary of all four-stackers, continued to sail until the hard years of the Depression in the early thirties. Her profitability reduced by fewer passengers on the Atlantic run to fill her berths and competition from the newer and faster breed of super-liners, the old *Mauretania* was repainted in white and sent on tropic cruises, even cheap trips to "nowhere." She was finally broken up in Scotland in 1935.

The *Olympic* met a similar fate in 1935–37. As with the *Mauretania,* some of her fittings were auctioned off and found their way to shoreside homes in hotels, restaurants, and pubs. The *Aquitania* survived through the next decade and was not dismantled until as late as 1950. The three big German liners all went to the Allies after World War I. The *Imperator* was handed

over to Cunard, mostly in compensation for the loss of the *Lusitania,* and was renamed *Berengaria.* She was immensely popular and survived until 1939, just as another war was erupting. The former *Vaterland* was seized by the Americans in 1917, and became the *Leviathan.* As the second largest liner of her time, she was alone in being quite unsuccessful. Among other problems, Prohibition kept her dry. She was laid up in 1934, a sad and sorry ship, and was finally sent to the scrappers in Scotland four years later. Lastly, the *Bismarck* was passed to the White Star Line and became their *Majestic.* She was the largest liner of the day (from 1922 through 1935). Nevertheless, she too fell on hard times during the Depression. White Star Line suffered financial collapse and merged with their sometime rival, Cunard, in 1934. *Majestic* was decommissioned by the renamed Cunard-White Star Line in 1937, and became a cadet training ship. Sadly, she burned out two years later and was scrapped in 1940, her remains then going to munitions factories to fight the very Germans who had created her. By then, of course, the era of those first floating palaces was long past.

The *Imperator* received raptuous praises from the very start. She did have, however, one serious technical blemish: she was top-heavy. Her reputation could have been ruined by such a flaw. Among other antidotes to her condition, her funnels were cut down. Somehow, it added to her overall appearance.

CHAPTER THREE

LINERS BETWEEN THE WARS

THE *ILE DE FRANCE* WAS THE FIRST LARGE LINER TO BE BUILT AFTER THE FIRST

World War. She was launched in 1926. There were other passenger ships built in the early twen-

ties, but they were either of prewar design or smaller size. The *Ile,* as she was fondly called, was

the first new big ship—in fact, the first of a new generation of superships. This new French ship

was not, however, intended to be the largest or fastest or, indeed, statistically superlative in any

way. Even her appearance, while fashioned after many earlier passenger ships, was not espe-

cially trendy. It was based on a prescribed formula: two tall masts and three funnels. The great

excitement was centered on her interior décor. There had never been a liner quite like her.

Earlier shipboard decoration copied shore styles: castles, manor houses, and English country

houses in the early days, followed by dabblings in the exotic—Arabian, Egyptian, and even

Moorish concoctions. The basic intent of those décors was to remind passengers of shore, even

After the horrors and the depletion of the first World War, the Germans miraculously rallied by the late twenties. Their new transatlantic team consisted of two of the finest superliners of all time, the *Bremen* and *Europa,* and one somewhat smaller and slower ship, the *Columbus.*

if they were coping with a violent ocean storm. The *Ile* represented a new age—she was an individual, a revolutionary, the trendsetter of her time. She inaugurated so-called "ocean liner style," early Art Deco on the high seas. Her style did not copy any land establishment or hotel-like setting, but was a floating luxury resort into itself. Soon, shoreside decorators would copy the ships, especially ones like the *Ile de France*.

Her creation, largely underwritten by the French government, which wanted another floating showcase, took place at the Penhoet shipyards of St. Nazaire. Again, great excitement and enthusiasm prevailed, not only at the yard, but throughout France. She would be spectacular, glittering, perhaps overwhelming. In June, 1927, while being readied for her maiden trip across to New York, she was opened for the first time to a curious public—and was given rave reviews. She was everything that those lavish preliminary brochures and flowing publicity sheets had promised.

The 390 first-class cabins were decorated in many different styles. Her public rooms were eclectic as well as spacious. She smoothly introduced a new age in liner design and décor, an era of angular and steel tubed furniture, sweeping columns and lacquered panels, glossy floors, indirect lighting, and such special distinctions as the longest bar afloat. The first-class restaurant, where there were no wood carved eagles or gilded angels, rose three decks in height and was closer in design to a stark Greek temple than those ornate concoctions of the turn of the century luxury liners. The main foyer was even higher—four decks to the ceiling—and the imitation Gothic chapel, surely the most remarkable of its kind, had 14 pillars. Every amenity was included—even a merry-go-round for the younger passengers.

The glorious *Ile de France* was part of a grand evolutionary plan begun by the French in 1912 with the *France*. The *Paris* followed, then the *Ile*, the *Lafayette, Champlain* and finally the flawless *Normandie*. With her spacious outer decks and magnificent innards, she was the ultimate liner.

Style, splendor, and a certain kind of ocean-going magic belonged to the *Ile de France*. She was one of the finest, most celebrated liners of all time. Even in her very final year, 1958, her tourist class menus still offered skate-in-butter sauce for breakfast!

The berthing was arranged for three classes: first, cabin, and an upgraded third. Steerage had virtually disappeared by the early twenties due to the newly enacted American Quota System, and liner companies were forced to create improved, far more comfortable third-class quarters instead, which were intended primarily for budget-minded tourists. The first-class section included such an unusually high number of suites and deluxe cabins that first class on the *Ile* was soon proclaimed as the very best of its kind on the sea. By 1935, she had carried more first-class travelers than any other liner. She was described by the legions of voyagers who preferred her ambience and style as "the cheeriest way to cross the North Atlantic."

The *Ile de France* was the first of a new breed of larger and more decoratively sumptuous Atlantic liners. She was also a contender in last great maritime race among the Europeans.

Most observers could not have expected that the Germans would soon rejoin the ocean liner sweepstakes, yet they did so in the early twenties. In 1918–19, they lost the "war to end all

*L*iner decoration was known for its extravangance, elegance, and often its novelty. Sometimes it was copied ashore. Salons, grill rooms, and music rooms were done in every possible style and period: Egyptian, Italian Renaissance, Moorish, Spanish. Louis XIV, XV and XVI, Empire, Georgian. Queen Anne: Jacobean, Tudor, Art Nouveau, Art Deco, even Bauhaus. Decorative ingredients included rare woods, handmade carpets, marble and mosaic, bronze, hammered glass, and custom-made Lalique and Wedgwood. Tapestries were especially woven and paintings deliberately commissioned.

wars," and were all but completely stripped of any decent passenger ships. Even that old four-stacker, the former *Deutschland,* still mechanically troublesome, was revived but as a demoded, austere migrant ship. Any new tonnage from the Germans would be necessarily more moderate and conservative. In 1924, Germany's new national flagship was the 32,500-ton (29,250 t) *Columbus.* A fine and solid ship, she was not distinctive in any way. The Germans were being very cautious, or so it seemed. But soon after she sailed away from the shipyards that built her to begin her first commercial sailings, her plans were left on the drawing boards. The Germans had planned for two more, quite similar, 35,000-ton (31,300 t) running mates. There was still a need for three liners to run a weekly schedule—one sailing from each direction and one in motion. But soon after the first sketches were completed, ambitions heightened and the specifications increased. The new German team would be at least 50,000 tons (45,000 t)— not quite the largest afloat, but within their hulls would be the most powerful steam turbine

NORDDEUTSCHER LLOYD BREMEN

WILH™ JÖNTZEN BREMEN

machinery to date. These would be the new German "monsters," proud successors to the *Kaiser Wilhelm der Grosse.* They would assuredly take the Blue Ribbon from Britain's *Mauretania.*

By the mid-twenties, the trend in liner design was toward squat stacks, intended to make the liners appear longer, sleeker, more stream-lined. *The Bremen and Europa appeared with extremely low funnels, in 1929-30, and were praised for their sense of modernity. However, too much smoke drifted onto the aft decks and the funnels had to be heightened.*

The very best German designers and engineers competed for the honor of creating these new national symbols, which were to be named *Bremen* and *Europa.* The hulls would be long and sleek with rounded stems intended to increase overall speed. Notably, they would introduce the bulbous bow, a new and quite novel design feature that, among other benefits, greatly reduced drag at sea. At times, the ships looked almost sinister, especially with their twin squat stacks (these were soon raised, however, because smoke and soot were falling on passengers resting in aft deck chairs).

As shipyard crews adhered to rigorous schedules (the *Bremen* was built at Bremen, the *Europa* at Hamburg), North German Lloyd publicists and very eager Berlin ministers, the benefactors of the new ships, produced a grandiose scheme: the two liners would cross to New York together and both would take the Ribbon from the British. They felt that the world would be impressed by Germany's recovery, skill, and technological might.

The two liners were launched a day apart, in August, 1928, but thereafter the plan went astray. Seven months later, in March, the *Europa*—while still being outfitted—was so badly damaged by a sudden fire that estimators initially recommended scrapping her. The necessary repairs would take a full year, so the simultaneous maiden voyages were cancelled. The *Bremen* went alone, the next July, and succeeded. She defiantly snatched the Blue Ribbon, making the run to New York in four days and 17 hours—two hours less than the *Mauretania's* record established 22 years earlier. While Berlin beamed, a congratulatory telegram was flashed from the old Cunarder to the new German liner.

As intended, the *Bremen* made headline news and reclaimed the maritime honors the Germans so desperately wanted. By being first, she also became the better known, and slightly more successful of this new pair. The *Europa* took the record in March, 1930, but the title later

went back to the *Bremen* before it passed to the new Italian *Rex* in the summer of 1933.

The British made the next move, in the spring of 1931, with the ultra luxurious *Empress of Britain*. She was one of the great dream boats—big, majestic, almost overpowering, and magnificent within. Like the French *Ile*, she was neither the world's largest nor fastest. However, she was an impressive flagship for her owners, the Canadian Pacific Company, and by far the largest liner ever on the Europe to Canada run. This was actually her most unique purpose: she was intended to be the luxuriously comfortable lure to both American and Canadian passengers who would sail in her from Quebec City on the St. Lawrence River. It was to be the new alternative in transatlantic travel. It was an interesting plan, but in reality, most passengers still preferred the customary routing through New York. Consequently, she was not quite as successful as hoped.

Her interiors were lavish. The Salle Jacques Cartier, the first-class restaurant, was finished in natural oak and ranked as the largest unpillared room at sea. Two private dining rooms, the Salle Montcalm and Salle Wolfe, were also provided. The 165-foot (49 m) long Mall, set out with

Canadian Pacific's *Empress of Britain* was one of the great dreamboats—the embodiment of the grand ocean liner. With three enormous buff funnels offset by an all-white hull, she appeared far larger than she actually was. Decoratively, she was equally stunning. Her Knickerbocker Bar, for example, included artwork that depicted the evolution of the cocktail.

chesterfields, armchairs, and deep pile rugs, connected some of the ship's lounges and salons. The Knickerbocker Bar included artwork that quite humorously depicted the evolution of the cocktail. Even the lower deck Olympian Pool was grand, featuring a glass ceiling that included artificial illumination, and was supported by rows of blue-colored pillars. Large turtles mounted at each end dispensed saltwater into the pool itself.

The big *Empress* had the novel distinction of being among the first of the large liners designed for cruising as well as transportation. Each winter when the Atlantic grew cold and often nasty, and the numbers of passengers declined considerably, Canadian Pacific, with considerable foresight, sent their 42,300-ton (38,070 t) flagship on leisurely and luxurious trips around the world. These would last as long as 125 days, leaving New York after Christmas and returning in the springtime. The routing became rather traditional: across to the Mediterranean, North Africa, and the Holy Land, through the Suez and into the Red Sea, India and Ceylon, Southeast Asia and the Dutch East Indies, China, Hong Kong, Japan, across to Hawaii, California, and finally through the Panama Canal back to New York. Minimum fare was $2,000, and the best top deck suite went for eight times that amount. Many passengers even brought along their own servants at $1,000 each.

While the *Empress of Britain* was not a government-sponsored ship but a purely commercial venture, she was, quite sadly, one of the least profitable liners of her time. Even her lavish winter cruises fell into the red, victims of the lingering Depression. She remained, of course, the grandest and most prestigious liner ever to sail on the Canadian run and was even selected

*C*elebrities were featured aboard almost all sailings of the major liners in the twenties and thirties. The Prince of Wales, later Edward VIII, and still later the Duke of Windsor, crossed in the Berengaria *in 1924, disguised as a "Lord Renfrew." His disguise failed, however, almost from the start of the voyage. Others included Will Rogers, Mary Pickford and Douglas Fairbanks, Rudolph Valentino, Gloria Swanson, Henry Ford, J P Morgan, Albert Einstein, and the Queen of Rumania. Commodore Vanderbilt was such a regular traveler that when he found his favorite suite on his favorite ship taken by someone else, he promptly booked it for the next ten years.*

to carry Britain's King George VI and Queen Elizabeth in 1939. There had been many rumors

that a sister ship was being planned, but Canadian Pacific was quick to deny them. One big liner

was quite enough.

Money-making problems would plague almost all of the big liners of the thirties. The

Queen Mary was the only exception—she had endearing qualities that evidently appealed to

the traveling public. This lack of profit also tarnished the otherwise splendid images of

Italy's twin contenders in the ocean liner races. Under the personal guidance and strict

instruction of Mussolini himself, a pair of ocean giants were delivered in 1932. While

there was widespread unemployment on both sides of the Atlantic and transoceanic trade

had slipped to its lowest ever numbers, both were expected to be champion ships. In fact, only

the *Rex* succeeded, and just for two years, 1933–35, when she was Italy's single Blue Ribbon

holder. Otherwise, the ships often sailed only half-full.

The *Rex* and her fleetmate, the *Conte di Savoia,* were quite different from each other. The

former, for example, was both larger and faster; the latter better looking and with slightly finer

appointments. Originally ordered by separate Italian shipowners, they became running mates

The *Conte di Savoia* was exceptionally fine-looking, with two rather large funnels placed forward, a series of decks that graduated aft, and a long, well proportioned black hull. She and her fleetmate, the *Rex*, were to push Italy to transatlantic prominence.

when Mussolini merged their owners, mostly to eliminate unneccessary competition and cut costs. The Italian Line's two liners were to herald a new era for the Mediterranean run, a route largely bypassed by Atlantic travelers, who tended to use the Northern passage. The Italians mounted a large, colorful campaign advertising the glories of the sunny southern route. The Italian Riviera, with its quaint little harbors and splendid beaches, was the main lure. On board these ships—the first to have several outdoor pools—sand was scattered around the lido decks to convey the appealing message, "The Riviera comes to meet you on board the *Rex* and *Conte di Savoia.*" There were rows of reclining deck chairs and colored umbrellas, and the stripe-shirted stewards catered to the passengers' needs. Indeed, the liners were not only floating hotels, but floating resorts as well.

Teething problems, such as the *Deutschland*'s vibrations and excessive rattling, and the *Imperator*'s instability in her maiden year, have often beset the most ambitious ships. In September, 1932, the *Rex* was still within the confines of the Mediterranean portion of her maiden voyage when, while approaching Gibraltar, her engines failed. She was crippled mechanically. The Italians were mortified. The ship had to wait three days for repairs and many of her passen-

gers grew impatient. The mayor of New York, Jimmy Walker, defected to the more reliable German *Europa* for his journey home.

Secretly, the Italians had been hoping to capture the Blue Ribbon on the maiden trip, but now that had to wait. Repairs became the priority. Once at New York, there were even more problems. The *Rex* sat, amidst celebratory parties, receptions, and tours, while a railroad tender supplied her with emergency power. Meanwhile, other Italian liners were speeding westward to deliver spare parts from the flagship's Genoa builders.

It took almost a year, but in August, 1933, the *Rex* captured the Ribbon. She took it from the *Bremen* with an average speed of 28.92 knots, making the run in four days, 13 hours.

The 48,500-ton (43,650 t) *Conte di Savoia* made her maiden trip two months after the *Rex*, in November, 1932. It all seemed to go quite well until, 900 miles west of the American mainland, an outlet valve below the waterline jammed and blew a very worrisome hole in the ship's hull. In a matter of minutes, seawater began to fill the ship's dynamo compartment. It was decided to keep the incident secret from the liner's otherwise excited passengers. Matters were, however, quite serious: inspections revealed that the 814-foot (244 m) liner could sink perhaps in as little as five hours. But the ship's staff was very resourceful and one crew member, exhibiting extraordinary bravery, went below and filled the hole with cement. The new Italian liner was safe and able to continue to New York. Later, the passengers were told of the man's heroism and a very substantial booty was collected and sent to that skillful crew member.

The Atlantic can be among the worst of passages. Travelers feared the effects of rough waters: a rolling ship, crashing tableware, and, deadliest of all, the uncomfortable, unmistak-

Both big Italians of the thirties had their distinctions. The *Conte di Savoia* was the "roll-less ship," the first superliner to have a gyro-stabilizer system. The *Rex* was a Blue Ribbon champ, the fastest liner ever to sail the sunny Mediterranean route.

able symptoms of *mal de mer*. Ship designers and owners worked hard to diminish these fears and to make their vessels sturdier, or at least to convince passengers that they were safer. Overshadowed by the earlier *Rex,* the *Conte di Savoia* needed her own identity, her own notation, and so she was "the roll-less ship." It was a repeat of the story of the *Olympic* and the *Titanic,* the latter of which needed a distinctive quality, and was therefore called "unsinkable." The *Conte de Savoia* was the first major liner to have a gyro-stabilizer system, a balancing system that predated the fin stabilizers that would appear in the 1950s. Word spread about the possibilities of "the smoothest sail on the Atlantic," but the system was successful only to a limited extent. It could not be used, for example, on westbound trips because of prevailing winds. Therefore, passengers were often unpleasantly surprised to find the liner tossing and pitching like other ships.

Three years after the debut of these Italian ships, the French produced a liner designed to pull out all the stops and take all the records. The exquisite *Normandie,* the most splendid of all superships in that era, was commissioned in the spring of 1935. Her creators had three goals: to build the first liner not only to exceed 1,000 feet (300 m) in length, but also to weigh at least 60,000 tons (54,000 t); to make the fastest ship on the Atlantic; and to create a dazzling, stun-

The two Italians had rather sad lives otherwise. They were never as popular and therefore not as profitable as their owners had expected, and their lives were prematurely shortened by the Second World War. Both ships sailed commercially for less than eight years.

The French Line's fabulous *Normandie* was a floating representative of French design. A detailed floor plan (right) gives some indication of her size and grandeur. The bronze statue, "La Normandie," executed specially by Beaudry for the ship, stood in the stairwell leading to the smoking room.

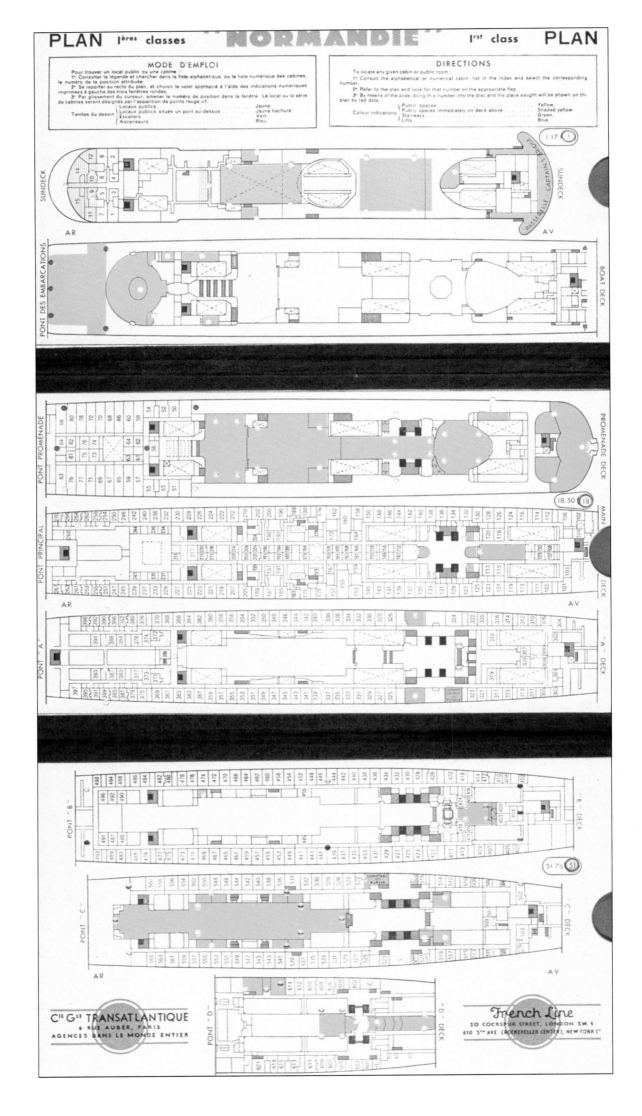

ning floating ambassador of French design, decoration, and technology. In all of these aims, the *Normandie* succeeded brilliantly.

Laid down in January, 1931, at the big shipyards at St. Nazaire, her schedule was delayed by the Depression. In many ways, she was a symbol of hope during those adverse times, but she was criticized as well, as "an expensive extravagance, inexcusable foolishness!" Rumors abounded that she might be named *Jean d'Arc, La Belle France,* or even *Maurice Chevalier*! However, she was launched as the *Normandie,* a ship so massive that the backwash of her 1028-foot (308 m) long unfinished hull was enough to sweep 100 shipyard workers into the Loire. Already, she was a ship of impact.

When complete, with her extraordinary profile capped by three enormous red and black funnels, the *Normandie*'s tonnage by far exceeded the 60,000 ton mark: she was finally placed at over 79,000 tons (71,100 t). As her French owners intended, she was the biggest liner in the world. But their triumph was short-lived. Word came from across the Channel, from those Scottish shipbuilders on the Clyde, that the first of a new team of record breakers being built by Cunard would be at least 80,000 tons (72,000 t). The *Normandie* would be in second place! Consequently, in the liner's first winter refit, in 1935–36, she was fitted with a large but unnecessary aft deckhouse. This pushed her tonnage to 83,400 tons (75,060 t). The new Cunarder, to be called *Queen Mary,* would be finished at 80,700 tons (72,630 t). The French had won—at least temporarily. The second Cunarder, the *Queen Elizabeth,* would be bigger still, at 83,600 tons (75,240 t). She would take the record for all time.

The *Normandie* swept across the Atlantic with a faster record than Italy's *Rex.* As planned, the French now had the Blue Ribbon as well. The *Normandie*'s average speed stood at 28.92 knots. But just little more than a year later, the brand new *Queen Mary* did 30.14 and grabbed the pennant. In the spring of 1937, the *Normandie* made another bid and won at 30.9 knots, followed by a record 31.2 the following summer. It began to seem as if the trophy would remain in Paris. Yet in August, 1938, the beloved *Queen Mary* proved the faster with an average speed of 31.6 knots. The French were finally beaten.

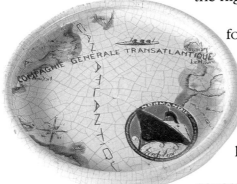

The *Normandie* looked different than most contemporary liners and was quickly acclaimed for her high sense of the *moderne*. She had a clean look: raked and well balanced, proof that design affects speed and performance. But of course it was her interior that received the highest praise, the accolades, the sighs, and lured the passengers. The main dining room, for example, was unlike anything yet seen at sea—a brilliant creation of bronze, hammered glass, and special Lalique fixtures. It sat 1000 diners, rose three decks in height, and offered menus that were beyond compare. The Winter Garden, with its tropical plants and lush greenery, included caged birds and sprays of water. The main lounge was covered by Dupas glass panels; the chairs were upholstered in specially made Aubusson tapestries. Like her Gallic predecessor, the superb *Ile de France,* each of the *Normandie*'s 400 first class cabins were decorated individually. Again, there was a string of deluxe cabins and suites, and even two premier sun deck apartments. Each of these consisted of a private terrace, four bedrooms, a living room, servant's quarters, and even a small private dining room. The indoor pool was even rather noteworthy: 80 feet (24 m) long with graduating levels of mosaic tiles.

And so, in her third intention, the *Normandie* was also successful: she was "the most lavish liner of her time."

Unfortunately, however, like Canadian Pacific's *Empress of Britain* and the two big Italian liners, the *Normandie* sailed mostly in the red. Often, she was only a half to two-thirds full. In retrospect, one problem was that she was so overly luxurious, so grandly pretentious, that her image often discouraged some of the very passengers that otherwise might have sailed in her. But like the *Bremen* and the *Rex,* the *Normandie* was underwritten largely by her government as a prestige piece. Perhaps high profit was never really a serious consideration. She succeeded in other ways, especially in creating an impression of floating magnificence.

Good, old, conservative Cunard was still the solid, comfort-conscious firm that they had been in that long-gone era of little paddlewheelers like the *Britannia* and her nine-and-a-half-day trips in 1840. Cunard also still believed in providing the most efficient and most precise service possible, not in records set for record's sake. They claimed that record runs and the Blue Ribbon were incidental to their passengers' comfort and safety. However, in the early thir-

The *Normandie* was decoratively the most magnificent liner of her time. Her main restaurant, for example, was a space of wondrous style: bronze and hammered glass, Lalique fixtures, and seating for 1,000. And all the wines were free! Her chapel could seat 100 and her array of suites included two penthouses with private sun decks.

ties, their Liverpool visionaries began to dream of the greatest transatlantic relay ever: the first

two-ship team to run weekly service from both sides of the Atlantic for most of the year. Obvi-

ously, such liners would have to be both very big and very powerful.

The plates for the first were laid two days after Chrismas, 1930. Cunard wanted a solid,

sensible, stately looking ship, and looked back at the plans for their illustrious and highly suc-

> *M*idnight sailings were rather common at New York in the years between the wars. Visitors went aboard several hours prior, some to see departing family or friends, and others just to have a dance in the ballroom—a night out!

cessful *Aquitania* of 1914. The new ship, with three instead of four funnels, and a majestic rake

and balance in her overall design, would be considerably less pretentious and less trendy than

the French *Normandie,* which was being built at the same time.

The Depression adversely affected this new Cunarder, just as it did the *Normandie.* The

project was stopped entirely by late 1931, and then almost cancelled. The great hull sat on the

ways—resting, lonesome, a nesting for birds. It seemed that only crews of watchmen were

about. Times were indeed hard: the transatlantic trade was greatly diminished, the predictions

for the future were far from bright, and company treasuries, even those of firms as rich as

Cunard, were being drained.

The *Normandie's* effect was far-reaching: interior decor, fashions, Hollywood, toys. She even inspired an entire hotel, which was named after her, in San Juan, Puerto Rico. She also lives on in other ways. Five medallions depicting the cities of Normandy are still used on the front doors of a small church in Brooklyn Heights, New York.

Over two years later, in April, 1934, the British Government decided to extend a substan-

tial loan to Cunard so that the new liner, to be called *Victoria,* could be finished. The Depres-

sion lingered and travel forecasts remained dim, but rivalry with the French and their new

Normandie produced the "go ahead" from London. Britain wouldn't easily let go of her top

standing on the Atlantic.

The launching was set for September, 1934. The highly secretive process of selecting a

suitable name produced a most interesting tale. It seemed that Cunard was interested in *Victo-*

ria, a royal name rather than the customary Roman province, but one which had the accepted

convention of ending in "ia." The story goes that the Cunard chairman approached King

Steamer poster art perhaps reached its highwater point in the thirties. Great artists, including France's Cassandre and Britain's Shoesmith, did considerable work for steamship firms. The *Normandie* was the subject of some of the finest works.

George V, the grandson of the late Queen Victoria, and requested permission to name "Britain's finest liner after her most illustrious Queen." His Majesty was said to have misunderstood and, in smiling enthusiasm, not even thinking of his grandmother, announced that his wife would be delighted. His wife was Mary, queen consort. And so, the name became the official choice. The queen herself, in the presence of the king, did the honors. She used a bottle of Australian wine to send the *Queen Mary* down the ways.

An economically battered Britain, suffering from mass unemployment and food queues, in the grip of a lingering gloom, saw the new superliner as a symbol of hope, and cause for national celebration. She would regain the transatlantic honors for her country and at the same time be one of the greatest ships to ply the ocean. In her 1018-foot (308m) long hull, there were 10,000,000 rivets, 2,000 portholes, and 2,500 square feet (225m²) of glass. She boasted 600 telephones and 700 clocks, and as many as 56 different kinds of wood were used throughout her vast interiors. While in some areas her décor leaned toward the Art Deco style of chromium rails, trumpet lamps, and glossy linoleum floors, she was generally a warm and inviting ship. Unmistakably, she was a British liner—with fireplaces and oversized chairs, lots of flowers, and ritual tea at four. Evidently, she had only one blemish: she was soon noted as a great roller at sea. Transoceanic gossips reported that "she could roll the milk out of a cup of tea."

The *Queen Mary* steamed into New York harbor for a tugboat-tooting welcome in May, 1936. It was a year after the *Normandie* had arrived. The new British liner excelled and captured the Blue Ribbon that same summer, but the aforementioned struggle between the new French liner and the British queen sent the record across the Channel a few times. Finally, in August, 1938, the Cunarder took the pennant firmly and thereafter remained the fastest line afloat for nearly 15 years. She was finally outraced by the last oceangoing recordbreaker, the brilliant *United States,* in 1952.

The stately *Queen Mary* was certainly not as glamorous as the *Normandie,* but she was more successful, with a warmer, cozy charm that would endear her to legions of travellers. Candy, cookie, and tobacco tins were splendid souvenirs. Included in this group (opposite page) are the Cunard *Queens,* the German sisters *Bremen* and *Europa,* the United States, the *Mauretania,* and the 1939 "queen of the South Atlantic route," the British *Andes.*

Adolf Hitler offered the Iron Cross and $250,000 to the U-boat commander who could sink either the Queen Mary *or* Queen Elizabeth *in wartime. On several occasions, for propaganda purposes, Nazi radio erroneously reported that the Queens had been destroyed.*

Cunard had planned to begin their first two-ship Atlantic shuttle in the spring of 1940, but

Hitler changed all that. The company's second superliner, a ship of different design (with two

instead of three funnels, for example) and slightly larger, was launched in the otherwise tense

weeks of the autumn of 1938. Simultaneously, there were the Hitler-Chamberlain meetings,

armament and annexation, and growing fears of another vast conflict. Originally to have been

named *King George V,* the new liner was more thoughtfully called *Queen Elizabeth* and was

baptized by the new queen of the same name. Her eldest daughter, the young Princess Eliza-

beth, was present at the ceremonies. Some 30 years later, a queen herself, she would name the

next Cunard superliner, the *Queen Elizabeth 2.*

The new *Elizabeth* did not take her commercial maiden voyage as planned in April, 1940.

In fact, months before and as Britain's urgent war machine was started, her final construction

and outfitting were halted. There were even proposals that she should be sold off to the Ameri-

cans. On the Clyde, warships now had priority. She remained at her builder's dock in that first

winter of war, but amidst increasing danger. Worrisome reports from intelligence agents

revealed that the Nazis planned to bomb or at least sabotage her and that German agents were

already in the Glasgow area. In response, Winston Churchill, then first Lord of the Admiralty,

ordered her away from British shores. A deliberate rumor was spread that the new *Queen*

would travel down to Southampton for drydocking. In doing so, she would have to pass

The liners at war!
Gone were the beauti-
ful exteriors, the luxu-
rious innards, the
familiar features of
peacetime. Cunard's
Queen Elizabeth
arrived on her maiden
voyage to New York,
in March 1940, in war-
paint. She wasn't even
accorded the tradi-
tional fireboat recep-
tions. It was all a
secret affair, a daring
escape from the Nazi
bombers that threat-
ened her birthplace in
Scotland.

through the English Channel. The Nazis, upon hearing this, planned to have Luftwaffe bombers waiting. Instead, soon after leaving the River Clyde, the *Elizabeth*—while still incomplete and with some unalerted shipyard crews still aboard—suddenly changed course and sped into the eastern Atlantic above Northern Ireland. The Nazis were livid—they had lost their chance. Westbound, blacked out, in the tightest secrecy, the liner traveled without revealing her destination, even to those on board. Many suspected Halifax. Instead, she went directly to New York, to Cunard's terminal at the foot of West 50th Street and there joined the laid-up *Queen Mary* and *Normandie*. Together for about two weeks, they were the three largest ocean liners ever built. The new *Elizabeth* had a unique maiden arrival. She came in coated in war paint, completely covered in grey. It was a rather solemn affair compared to the joyous welcomes usually reserved for such liners, those noisy receptions for which New York harbor was so well-known.

The liners did their most heroic work in wartime. Most were converted to troopships, but others were redone as attack cruisers, hospital ships, floating repair plants, even sinister prison ships.

Soon, the *Queens* were outfitted as troopships—the biggest of all time, carrying as many as eight times their normal capacity (the *Mary* has the highest record of all ships, 16,683 troops on a wartime crossing in 1943). They were sent off on urgent voyages, covered in grey, blacked out, and often with radio silence, and were superbly successful. The two big Cunarders were

aptly applauded after the Second World War: "Together, they helped to win the war in Europe by at least a year."

The war years were, of course, extremely destructive and disruptive. The *Bremen* was set afire by an unhappy crewmember while she was lying at her Bremerhaven berth in March, 1941. A mighty and distinctive ship, Germany's last record breaker, her remains were later cut up and sent to Nazi munitions plants. The *Europa* lingered in home waters, all but forgotten, and during the Allied invasion, in spring 1945, she was surrendered to the Americans, who later gave her to the French. She was resurrected in 1950 as the *Liberté*. The *Empress of Britain*, attacked by enemy bombers and then torpedoed, sank in the eastern Atlantic in the fall of 1940. She was the largest Allied merchant ship loss. Both the big Italians were finished as well—the *Rex* was

bombed south of Trieste in September, 1944; the *Conte de Savoia* ended her days a year earlier,

not far from Venice. Finally, the brilliant *Normandie* had the most unexpected demise of all:

she burned and then capsized in the very confines of New York harbor, at her original French

Line berth, in February, 1942. Her greatly reduced remains were scrapped in 1946–47.

Most fortunately, the *Queens* survived intact. The heroic ships were returned unharmed to

Cunard for restoration. A little later than originally planned, the two-ship weekly service began

in the summer of 1947. They would become the most successful team ever to sail the Atlantic.

The cherished *Ile de France* was back as well by 1949, refitted, modernized, and sporting two

instead of three funnels.

One other dream boat from the years between the wars is worthy of mention. The Dutch

Nieuw Amsterdam, completed in 1938 and dubbed Holland's "ship of peace" (there were abso-

lutely no provisions made in her construction for possible wartime use), she was also pro-

claimed the "ship of tomorrow." Her superb Art Deco interiors were inspired in part by the

1933 World's Fair and would later feature touches from the 1939 Fair, staged at New York. The

36,200-ton (32,580t) liner included lighting fixtures of Venetian glass, pieces of carved ebony,

and a ceiling of Moroccan leather. The main restaurant was a fantastic creation of ivory walls,

pale gold ceiling, columns covered in gold leaf, tinted mirrors, satinwood furniture, and two-

tone carpeting. This ship also survived the war years and returned to the Atlantic in the late

forties after extensive trooping duties. The *Nieuw Amsterdam* then joined a virtually new fleet

of Atlantic liners, a new cast of glorious players.

The war was over and the liners were back! It took tremendous effort to revive them, often requiring hand-made equipment such as door hinges. But a boom was on in the late forties and fif-ties—a new genera-tion of tourists was travelling, prompting the speedy return of older ships as well as a fleet of new ones. Triumphant, the "new look" *Ile de France* arrives on her first postwar trip, in sum-mer 1949.

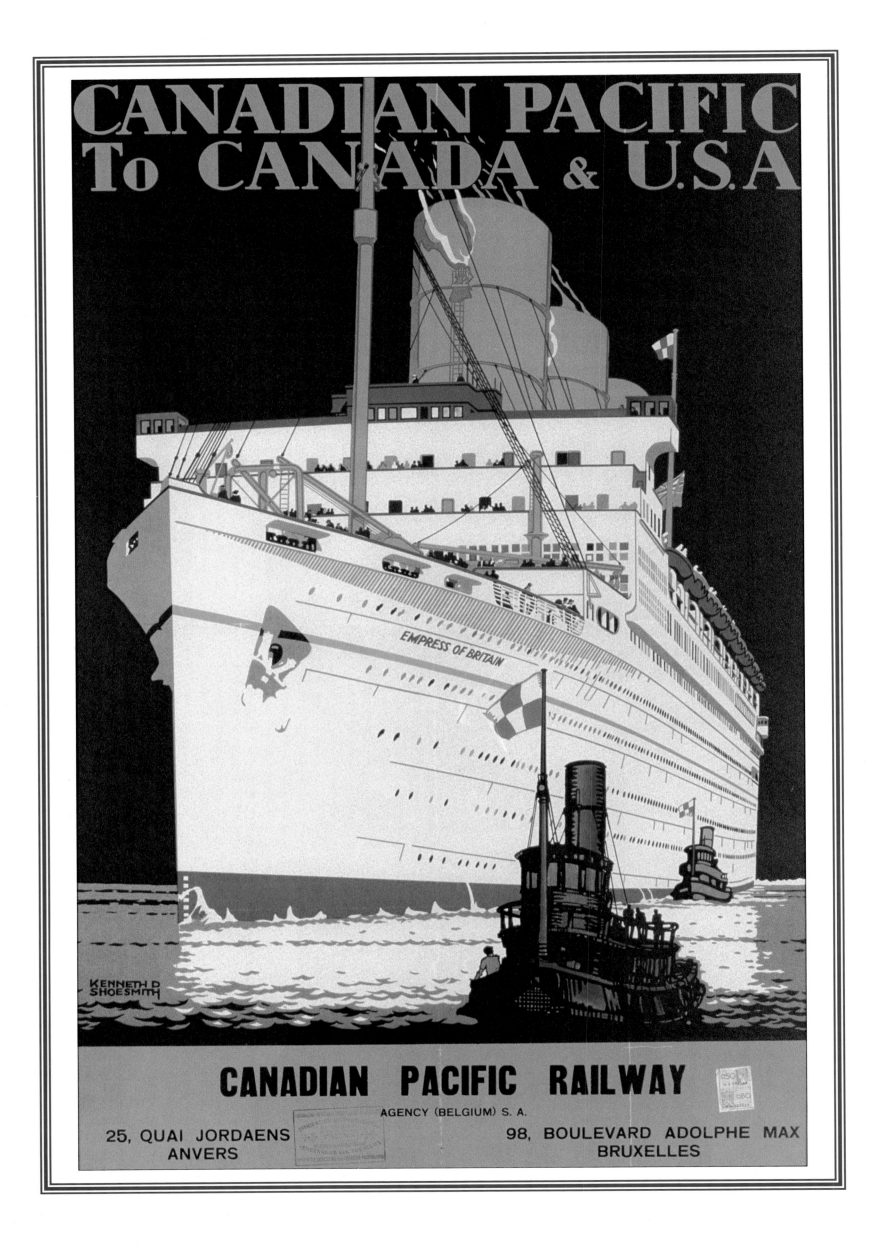

ATLANTIC TWILIGHT

The TRANSATLANTIC TRADE BOOMED FOR A FULL DECADE FOLLOWING THE END of the Second World War. A new prosperity brought new travelers and, inevitably, new ships. Generally, however, the era of the superliner races, those maritime sweepstakes waged mostly between the European nations, was over. The challenge for the Blue Ribbon and even those spirited contests for "world's largest" and "world's longest" were now far more restricted, perhaps even less enthusiastic, surely more limited. The Ribbon was still held by Cunard's *Queen Mary,* and the distinction of "largest" was retained by that other mighty Cunarder of the time, the *Queen Elizabeth.*

Both the Germans and the Italians were now out of the running, having suffered severe war losses. The Germans were unable to even resume passenger service until as late as the mid-fifties and then only with a moderately sized, secondhand ship. The Italians opted to rebuild with far more conservative tonnage, with nothing larger than 30,000 tons (270,000 t) for some years to come. Even the French were somewhat less inspired. Their only large prewar survivor, the superb *Ile de France,* was joined by that former German ship, the onetime champion

Canadian Pacific's magnificent *Empress of Britain* was the last large liner built by that company. Sadly, she was sunk during the Second World War.

Europa of 1930, restyled as the *Liberté*. Canadian Pacific would never again build a large *Empress* for their St. Lawrence River trade and the Dutch would spend over a decade contemplating a suitably sized running mate to their glorious prewar *Nieuw Amsterdam*.

Ironically, since they had previously shown little desire to enter the races, it was the Americans who produced the most important Atlantic superliner of the postwar era. She was the brilliant *United States*. Previously, the United States Line seemed content with medium-sized ships (with the exception of the giant *Leviathan* of the twenties and thirties, which was actually

an inherited ship—a German war prize from 1917). The decision to build the first brand-new Yankee supership was sparked by two considerations: the potential for commercial profit from the buoyant North Atlantic trade, and perhaps even more importantly, the need for a wartime troopship. (In later years, and because of her rather somber, almost austere, less-than-luxurious accommodations, it was often said that the *United States* was actually a full-time troopship disguised as a passenger liner.) The military interest in her construction was a result of the success of the two Cunard *Queens* as wartime troop transports. Underwritten largely by the Americans, each of those British ships carried in excess of 15,000 soldier-passengers and could deliver them with amazing speed and reliability. Military sponsors in Washington wanted a potential troopship of their own and so, in joint effort with the United States Lines, underwrote what would become the most technologically advanced superliner of her time. In fact, the government would pay for nearly 70 percent of the ship's exceptional $78 million cost.

The Pentagon insisted on three prime ingredients in the new supership: extraordinary safety, amazing speed, and of course, quick and easy convertibility from commercial liner to

New liners steadily rolled off the ways in the 1950s. America built the most technologically advanced, the brilliant *United States*, the last Blue Ribbon champion. She was followed by a new Swedish flagship that had all-outside cabins, a Dutch flagship without traditional smokestacks, and an Italian flagship that was convertible to nuclear-power.

military troopship. For safety, there were "defense" features almost equivalent to those found

on a complete and major warship. There was, for example, an abnormally high fuel capacity,

subdivisions of watertight compartments, and even two separate engine rooms, one of which

could function alone and still maintain maximum power and speed should the other be hit by a

torpedo. Also, no ship was as fireproof. More aluminum was built in her than in any other

creation, either ashore or afloat. Even the artwork and the draperies were specially fire-

retardant. Wooden picture frames were not permitted on board even for crew members—they

had to be done in aluminum. It became well-known that "the only wood aboard the *United*

States was in the butcher's block and the piano." Actually, the ship's genius designer, William

Francis Gibbs, had rigorously argued with the Steinway Company to get them to produce an

aluminum piano. The firm steadfastly refused.

The *United States* was the very last Blue Ribbon champion. Her actual top speed, like most of her special design components, was kept a secret for some years after her completion. It was eventually revealed that for a short time during her trials, in June 1952, she actually managed an extraordinary 38.25 knots. Her slender 990-foot (297 m) long hull registering only 53,000 gross tons (47,700 t), and with a razor-sharp bow and a low superstructure capped by two very large, but raked, funnels clearly reinforced the theory that design does indeed affect performance. That July, she wrested the Ribbon from the *Queen Mary* with absolute ease. The new American's top speed was recorded at over 38 knots, some seven knots faster than the Cunarder. And so, the honors went to a ship flying the Stars and Stripes for the first time in nearly a century, since those Collins Line ships mentioned in Chapter One. It would also be the last time that the trophy would change hands. No other liner would be faster—there would be no need.

The *France* was called the best French restaurant in the world by at least one epicure. The champagne and the caviar flowed, and there was still the choice of skate-in-butter sauce for breakfast in tourist class.

In October, 1958, a mere six years after the *United States* was first commissioned, the first commercial jet flew the North Atlantic. Suddenly and abruptly, transatlantic travel time became six hours instead of six days. The differences were irresistable, even to liner loyalists. Within six months, the airlines secured two-thirds of all transatlantic travel. Within less than a decade, more than 95 percent would go by air. Consequently, the sixties in particular proved to be largely ruinous for transatlantic shippers. Winter crossings dwindled until they were all but nonexistent, fleets were reduced and staff cut, and by the end, in those final summer seasons, those vast lounges, ornate salons, and orderly promenades had grown very desolate. Even the illustrious *Queens* fell on hard times. On one crossing, the *Elizabeth* steamed into New York harbor with a scant 200 passengers being looked after by 1,200 crew members. The *Mary* was finally retired in 1967, and then went on to a different rest of sorts in southern California, serving as a museum and hotel ship; the *Elizabeth,* while being converted for new life as a roving university-cruise ship, burnt out in Hong Kong harbor in 1972. But, despite the inroads, the ravages even, made by the airlines, the age of the superliner—those big and lavish and powerful passenger ships—was not entirely over. Four were built in the 1960s.

The *France* was the last superliner to be built solely for the North Atlantic. The growing trend of off-season winter cruising to the warmer and more lucrative tropics was barely yet a consideration. The new Gallic flagship first appeared in New York to a noisy welcome of serenading tugs, spraying fireboats, and whirling helicopters, in the winter of 1962. It might have been too late, but there were at least a few more good years left for the French liner, another of those highly reputed, impeccably run, gourmet luxury ships flying the tricolor. That prized distinction remained true, "More seagulls follow the French liners than any others because the scraps of food are better!"

The *France* took four years, three months, and 28 days to complete, in the same dockyard at St. Nazaire that built the earlier *France,* the *Ile de France,* and the *Normandie.* The new ship was, like the great ships of the thirties, underwritten by her government, which was deeply concerned about the loss of colonial Algeria. The building of a national superliner was seen as a morale builder, another floating public relations piece. Initial studies concluded that one 66,000-ton (59,400 t) liner would be far superior to two, more conventional 30,000 tonners (27,000 t) and that a two-class ship, first and tourist, was preferable to the customary three-class system. Furthermore, with her capacity divided between some 500 in first class and about 1,500 in tourist class, the tourist section would have full decks, from stem to stern, and include choice center-ship areas that were traditionally allocated to first class. Her overall design would make her 1,035 feet (310 m) in length, the longest liner ever built—four feet longer than the *Queen Elizabeth* and seven feet longer than the *Normandie.*

After the first transatlantic jet crossing, in October 1958, it became official: the *United States* was the last liner to hold the Blue Ribbon. While there was a subsequent rumor that the *France*, in 1962, and then the *Queen Elizabeth 2*, in 1969, would make attempts, racing across the Atlantic was no longer worth the effort. Additional time at sea actually became desirable.

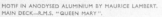

MOTIF IN ANODYSED ALUMINIUM BY MAURICE LAMBERT.
MAIN DECK—R.M.S. "QUEEN MARY".

R.M.S. "QUEEN MARY"   Thursday, June 10, 1937

GOOD MORNING!

Breakfast

FRUITS

Fresh Strawberries and Raspberries with Cream
Compôte of Prunes   Stewed Rhubarb   California Figs in Syrup
Grape Fruit   Pears   Bananas   Baked Apples
Apples   Tangerines   Oranges   Dried Figs
Honey Dew Melon   Cantaloup   Water Melon
Juices—Orange   Tomato   Grape Fruit   Prune

CEREALS

Oatmeal   Quaker Oats   Cream of Wheat   Wheatena
Hominy   Bonny Boy Toasted Oats   Farina   Post Toasties
Pep   Force Whole-Wheat Flakes   Shredded Wheat
Rice Krispies   Bran Flakes   Grape Nuts

TO ORDER—(10 minutes)—Onion Soup Gratinée

FISH

Fried Porgies and Lemon   Grilled Halibut Maître d'Hôtel
Kippered Herrings   Findon Haddock in Cream

EGGS AND OMELETTES

Eggs—Boiled, Turned, Fried, Poached, Scrambled and Indienne
Shirred Eggs Aurore   Omelettes: Spanish, Cheese, Plain

ENTREES

Minced Chicken Créole   Chipped Beef in Cream

GRILLS

Ham Steaks and Chutney Sauce   Lamb's Liver and Bacon
Tomato and Oxford Sausage   Mushrooms on Toast
Pale and Smoked Wiltshire, American and Irish Bacon
York and Wiltshire Ham

POTATOES

Creamed and German Fried

COLD MEATS ASSORTED

SALADS

Tomatoes   Chicory   Watercress   Spring Onions   Radishes

CAKES

Buckwheat   Griddle   Waffles   Maple or Golden Syrup

BREAD, Etc.

French   Graham   Brioche   Crescents   Oatcake
Rolls   Currant   Hovis   Cottage   Corn   Triscuits
Soda Scones   French Toast   Sultana Buns
Preserves   Honey   Marmalade

BEVERAGES

Tea: Indian, China, Ceylon, Linden and Camomile   Coffee
Cadbury's Cup Chocolate   Horlick's Malted Milk: Plain or Chocolate
Cocoa   Ovaltine   Instant Postum   Kaffee Hag Coffee

*Passengers on Special Diet are requested to make known their requirements
to the Head Waiter*

Cunard
White Star

PRINTED IN ENGLAND. Q.C.B.2.

A section of Doris Zinkeisen's main Painting in the Verandah Grill, Sun Deck, R.M.S. "Queen Mary".

R.M.S. Queen Mary
CUNARD WHITE STAR

Dining aboard the transatlantic liners, even as late as the 1950s, was a unique experience. Cunard, for example, proudly proclaimed that they could prepare a full breakfast in late afternoon or a full supper well after midnight. They would also meet all tastes—perhaps the only exception was when a Texas oil baron requested rattlesnake for dinner and there was none in the freezers. Even breakfast was expansive and included no less than eight different varieties of bacon.

Like most superliners before her, the *France* dazzled the public. Her interiors received particular praise though they were starkly modern in style, even, in ways, rather functionally cold. There was a splendid array of suites in first class, including some with private deck space and others with individual dining rooms and adjacent warming kitchens. Kennels on the sun deck had 20 separate compartments, all of them carpeted, having running water, and featuring special pet menus sent to their passenger-owners. The walkways even included a New York City fire hydrant and a Paris milestone. The theater on two levels could seat as many as 664 passengers, and there were two swimming pools, one below deck and the other in the stern section but protected by a glass shield. The first-class restaurant, the Chambord, was of circular design, used soft indirect lighting, boasted a glasslike main stairwell as an entrance, and could comfortably seat 400 at a time. Adjacent was a smaller, more intimate grill room, said to be the best French restaurant anywhere. Most of her staterooms, unlike most other transatlantic liners, included at least one private shower and toilet.

Especially in her maiden season, interested travelers and visitors alike were deluged with those statistics so long favored by steamship company public relations offices. There were, for example, over 25,000 linen sheets on board, 246,000 napkins, 47,500 pieces of silverware and, so it was estimated, if all 23,700 plates were stacked in a column they would measure 820 feet (246 m), or more than New York's Woolworth Building.

On her maiden voyage, in June 1960, the Italian *Leonardo da Vinci* was said to represent the future: she was designed to be convertible to nuclear power. An interesting idea, it never quite came to pass and by her end, in the mid-seventies, the *da Vinci* was both mechanically expensive and troublesome. She was the forerunner, however, in 1965, to the twins *Michelangelo* and *Raffaello*. Bigger and more lavish still, and persisting with steam turbines, they were too late for the Atlantic and never earned a cent in profit.

By 1974, 12 years after her maiden run, the *France*—like most of the remaining Atlantic liners—was at its worst. Passengers had steadily decreased and profits had greatly diminished; operational costs, particularly for fuel oil, had tripled in price. The French government would have to extend its annual operating subsidy from $14 to $24 million. Underwriting the new supersonic Concorde jet seemed a better investment, and so the subsidy was cut entirely. Without this vital assistance, even if the *France* was filled to the very last tourist class upper bunk, she was well beyond the means of the French Line. Near the very end, in September, 1974, some crew members mutinied off Le Havre, holding the giant liner at anchor in the English Channel while demanding that she be restored and at the same time asking for 35 percent wage increases. It was all hopeless. Soon, the *France* was recovered and sent to the backwaters of Le Havre, her home port, to await disposition. Some thought she might even be sold for scrap. And so, another once great Atlantic liner firm, the French Line, ended its transoceanic service.

Three years after the *France* was delivered, the Italians had added not one but twin superliners for their Mediterranean service. They were far too late and, in fact, never saw a day's profit in their decade of service. Several years earlier, in 1960, the Italian Line had boasted six liners, all of them medium-sized, including the brand-new *Leonardo da Vinci,* on the run to New York. The forecasts for the future had seemed bright and the Italians wanted their share of the profits.

The twin superships were the first pair of large liners to be built since the *Bremen* and *Europa* of 1929–30. The first of these to be launched was the *Michelangelo,* which was christened at Genoa in September, 1962; the *Raffaello* followed from a shipyard at Monfalcone on the Adriatic. They were delivered in the spring and summer of 1965 respectively. The *Michelangelo* was considered the flagship and together the two ships represented an investment of some $100 million. The sisters, although lighter at 45,000 tons (40,500 t) due to the extensive use of more modern materials such as aluminum, ranked as the longest Italian liners ever built at 902 feet (271 m) each, exceeding the 51,000-ton (45,900 t) *Rex's* 879 feet (264 m).

The new twins boasted unusual profiles. Their hulls were painted entirely in white, a departure from the customary black hull coloring of most Atlantic liners, and a wide green stripe was painted all around. Because of the length of the hulls and the coloring, the superstructure appeared to be lower and flatter than it actually was. In fact, it reached five decks above the main deck. The two funnels were positioned farther aft than usual and it might even have appeared that there was space for a third funnel as well. In fact, the forward space was deliberately created for an extensive first-class pool and lido area. The two 45-foot (13 m) high funnels were unique in themselves, being strongly reminiscent of the old birdcage masts aboard early battleships. Capped by long smoke-deflecting tops, the funnels were actually lattice cages that surrounded exhaust pipes.

These medallions were given out to passengers as souvenirs of the voyage, or "ricordo di viaggio."

The ships each had a full capacity for 1,775 passengers, and were divided into the traditional three classes: first, cabin, and tourist. Every cabin in all three classes had private facilities. In all, there were 30 public rooms, which included a 489-seat theater. Gone were the marbles, the ornate ceilings, and the columned lounges of the earlier *Rex* and her running mate, the *Conte di Savoia;* instead decorations used formica, ceramics, and specially created tapestries. Each ship had six separate swimming pools, of which three were deliberately shallow for the younger travelers. The three larger pools were infra-red heated so that passengers could lounge nearby even on chilly days at sea.

The initial hopes that the *Michelangelo* and *Raffaello* would enjoy long and profitable lives were far from correct. By 1970, both ships were losing money at an embarrassing rate. On some occasions, the 775 crew members outnumbered the fare-paying guests. There was talk of actually keeping the liners in service through a series of cost-trimming plans, but little was actually done and in each successive season the ships showed mounting losses. Italian seamens' strikes became more and more common as the government hinted of subsidy cuts and eventual withdrawal. Consequently, the liners were hard-pressed to maintain their published schedules and so alienated even the few remaining passengers.

The sharp rise in fuel costs in 1973 was another blow. The Italian government finally withdrew its support and both ships were laid up by the summer of 1975. Initially, the ships were moored at Genoa, but later were transferred to La Spezia, a smaller port and the home of the Mediterranean's biggest and busiest scrapyard. Newspaper reports began to hint that it was not inconceivable that the two superships would be scrapped, pathetically, on their tenth birthdays. The government was harshly criticized for building them in the first place.

Deficit-ridden, out-of-work ocean liners have often been the subjects of all sorts of proposals and the *Michelangelo* and *Raffaello* were no exceptions. Speculation about their futures included reports that they would become floating cancer clinics, hotels, even Soviet cruise ships. Instead, in 1977, they were sold to the Iranian government, which intended to use them as military barracks ships. They ended in more distant, Eastern waters: the *Raffaello* was sunk in an Iraqi air rad in 1983; the *Michelangelo* was finally sold off to Taiwanese shipbreakers four years later. By then, they were among the very last survivors of the once glorious Italian Line.

Ironically, but appropriately, it was the historic Cunard Company that created the last Atlantic superliner. She remains the only survivor of this illustrious transoceanic breed. In the early sixties, while still not totally sure of the future of transatlantic passenger-ship travel, Cunard directors, as always steeped in the conservative and the traditional, decided to replace the aging *Queen Mary.* They envisioned a large liner that would, among other things, carry the traditional three classes and work alongside the other vintaged *Queen Elizabeth.* This new design was dubbed *Q3,* the third *Queen.* It was a plan that needed very serious rethinking. Certainly the era of the three-class ship was past, and perhaps more importantly, a two-ship partnership with the original *Elizabeth* was misguided. Simply, there would no longer be a need for two big liners under the same house flag in regular Atlantic relay, except perhaps—and then only for a few more seasons—at the height of the tourist trade in summer. What then would Cunard do with two very large liners for the remaining nine or so months of each year?

Perhaps the closing of the curtain on the traditional North Atlantic liner trade was best signified, in 1967-68, with the final passages of the Cunard Queens. Like the *Elizabeth* (shown below), they went off to fireboat sprays, bagpipe serenades, and nostalgic tears.

While the *Elizabeth* was modernized and refitted in an attempt to make her ready to sail the tropics, she was simply too old and too expensive for such a transition. An open-air pool had been added in the stern, colored lights strung about, and at least one lounge refaced with loud colors and plastic flowers, but these surface alterations could not make an "indoor" Atlantic liner into an "outdoor" tropical cruise ship. Cunard needed a brand new ship that could sensibly divide her time most profitably: half the year on the waning Atlantic, half in the ever more popular sunny tropics. The grand old *Queen Mary,* tired and debt-ridden, was retired in 1967, and the *Elizabeth* soon followed. Earlier plans had suggested keeping her about, and on the Atlantic run no less, until as late as 1975. But those older *Queens,* surely faded dowagers by then, had passed their best. More importantly, Cunard scrapped the *Q3* plans—she too was outmoded and so never left the drawing board.

The new superliner, quickly dubbed *Q4,* was a far more enlightened blending of Atlantic liner and leisure cruise ship. Above all else, however, she would be a floating hotel, a comfortable, luxuriously fitted resort that moved. A rigidly class-divided, dark wood-paneled, basically indoor Atlantic steamer was completely part of the past. Of the new age of transatlantic passengers, few still wanted the columned salons and wood-panelled libraries; many more wanted shopping arcades, discos, and Las Vegas-style revues in those once-sedate main lounges that were now trimmed in stainless steel and formica rather than burl and tapesteries. There would only be two classes, first and tourist, and the distinctions would be far less noticeable. Certainly, tourist class—or transatlantic class, as Cunard redubbed it—was never quite as comfortable.

The first keel plates were laid down at the same Clydeside shipyards in Scotland that produced the previous *Queens* and the earlier *Lusitania* and *Aquitania,* in June, 1965. She would, of course, be a big ship, although not quite as large as either of the first *Queens,* and she would be powerful, although not a record breaker. Her profile would be far different, supposedly the next step in the evolution of big ship design. Only a single mast would be fitted above the bridge, the bow would be sharply raked, and the stern deck area rounded. On her white superstructure, in the new coupling of Madison Avenue advertising and steamship operations, the name Cunard would be spelled out in large red letters. This was necessary because one of the great staples of ocean liner recognition, the funnel colors, were to disappear completely with this new *Queen.* The single exhaust, a wide contraption capped by a slender smoke-emitting pipe, was to be painted only in black and white. Those well-established, thoroughly appealing funnel colors were simply not to be used. Cunard wanted to market itself in a new way, to avoid the past, and its conservative heritage. Instead the company wanted a new image—Cunard as a very contemporary firm in the age of floating resort-hotels in a far more modern Britain. (Ironically, years later, in 1982, Cunard would take a renewed and far more serious interest in its solid past and, among other touches, add those funnel colors on their flagship.)

> *The* Queen Elizabeth 2 *has been the most publicized big liner of all time. Her very existence in this jet-dominated age has made her, of course, the subject of curiosity. Despite her high sense of luxury, the extravagance of her first class quarters, and the opulence of her winter world cruises, she's had her share of woes. In 1972, for example, she endured a mid-Atlantic bomb hoax and a year later she was the subject of a threatened submarine attack by Arab terrorists during a celebratory cruise to Israel. Worse still, in April 1974, she was "immobilized" by engine troubles while cruising off Bermuda.*

Despite the inroads made by the airlines and some otherwise gloomy forecasts on the remaining future of transatlantic travel, Cunard persisted and built one last liner, the *Queen Elizabeth 2* of 1969. Her Majesty the Queen used the same pair of golden christening scissors that were used by her mother when she named the *Queen Elizabeth,* and by her grandmother when she named the *Queen Mary.*

The QE2 is, of course, the floating hotel. Every conceivable amenity is onboard, from posh grill rooms to a shopping mall, glass-covered pools, and closed circuit television. There are Las Vegas-style revues and a guest lecture program, health spa-type dining, and even conference rooms for business travellers.

The naming of the new liner was again a matter of considerable rumor. There were varied reports that she would be *Queen Mary II,* then *Britannia, Great Britain, William Shakespeare,* even *Winston Churchill.* The final decision was kept a tight secret until the very end and was the result of an agreement between Cunard and her Majesty Queen Elizabeth II, who had, like her grandmother, Queen Mary, and her mother, Queen Elizabeth, before her, consented to launch Britain's best-known ocean liner. On September 20, 1967, two days before the old *Queen Mary* was to leave New York on her very last Atlantic crossing, the new ship was named *Queen Elizabeth 2.*

Her maiden voyage was scheduled for January, 1969, three months after the original *Elizabeth's* last passage from New York. It seemed that it was all very carefully and thoughtfully timed. Actually, there was such demand—and ensuing publicity—that Cunard actually planned five separate trips for the new *Queen,* all of them said to be her "maiden voyage." The routing was different than any previous Atlantic supership: from Southampton across the mid-Atlantic to the sunny Caribbean and then northward to New York. Reservations were plentiful and included a good number of loyalists to both Cunard and the great age of the liners.

The *QE2,* as she was nicknamed, left her birthplace two months earlier, in November, for her first sea trials, but then quickly encountered serious turbine problems and other embarassing defects. Humiliated, she crept back to the John Brown shipyards. Cunard refused delivery. Thought to be repaired, she finally put into Southampton, her home port (again differing from the Liverpool registry for the old *Mary* and *Elizabeth*) and the location of Cunard's new, greatly streamlined headquarters, just after the New Year holidays. Embarassingly, more problems

were uncovered and once again Cunard refused their $80 million, 65,800-ton (59,220 t) ship. Worse still, those celebratory maiden voyages had to be cancelled, with the resulting delays costing over $10 million. She did not officially join the Cunard fleet until mid-April and the maiden trip, reset as a direct run from Southampton to New York, took place a month later.

The new *Queen's* only superliner companions were two other members of that once mighty and legendary group, the speedy *United States* and the renowned *France.* She would outlast both of them and, after 1974, when the French flagship was finally decomissioned, the Cunarder was alone. At that time, there was barely an alternate Atlantic passenger ship about. Her success on the transoceanic run has actually increased since then. There seem to be more and more travelers who want to enjoy the comforts of a five-day ocean passage. In 1987–88, Cunard invested over $160 million (more than twice her original construction cost some 20 years before) in what has been called "the most publicized liner afloat." She was redecorated and upgraded, more suites were added, the restaurants redone, and at least one grill room extended, but mostly, and through a very extensive mechanical conversion from those often troublesome, increasingly costly steam turbines to far more efficient diesel electric, her longevity has been extended—she should last well into the next century. Alone, the very last of her kind and a grand successor to that first *Britannia,* those turn of the century German record breakers, the *Lusitania* and the immortal *Titanic,* the exquisite *Normandie* and that final Blue Ribbon champion, the *United States,* the *Queen Elizabeth 2* seems to have a bright future. Surely, part of her great appeal lies in her historic position. She is the last of the Atlantic ocean liners.

DISASTERS: THE LOST LINERS

DISASTERS HOLD A VERY SPECIAL INTEREST, AND INTRIGUE EVEN, FOR MANY.

Certainly, one of the most enduring tragedies, and obsession to some, was the sinking of one of

the greatest and largest ocean liners of her time, the *Titanic.* Her loss during her maiden trip to

New York remains to this day the subject of further investigation and research, of new books

and now, with the discovery of the ship's remains on the floor of the western Atlantic, of video

documentaries. She lies there for all to see (in this marvelous age of robotic cameras) broken in

half, minus her funnels and masts, encrusted, decayed, and eroding, but in her own way an

extraordinary memento of that era of exceptional Atlantic liners.

The *Titanic* was to be the most important ship of 1912. Her owners, the White Star Line,

were proud of their great new ship, but knew quite well that in this ferociously competitive

maritime period her moment in the sun would be short-lived. Within a year, the Germans

The *Atlantique,* a splendidly appointed liner that was built for the South Atlantic crossing from Bordeaux to Rio and Buenos Aires, was destroyed by a massive fire in 1933.

would have a far larger and perhaps even grander liner. Consequently, the *Titanic* needed a

very special niche that would differentiate her from the other liners and would lure more pas-

sengers aboard. White Star and her Belfast builders set out to make her the safest ship afloat—

"unsinkable." She could stay afloat even if two of her 16 watertight compartments were

flooded, and far more dramatically, she would not even need the usual lifesaving gear. She

would carry lifeboats for only half her passengers.

Tremendous excitement surrounded her maiden trip, set for April, 1912. The millionaire

set were particularly fascinated and quite happy to pay nearly $5,000 for a first-class suite

aboard the inaugural run of the newest and largest of the "floating palaces." She set off on April

10, carrying a total of 2,207 passengers and crew, and sped quite briskly across the North Atlan-

tic. She was due along New York's West Side on the 16th. There seemed barely a dent in the

cheer and merriment onboard. Iceberg warnings, including ones sent by the big German liner

Amerika, went largely ignored. Even against icebergs the *Titanic* was thought to be invincible.

She couldn't sink.

Fate seemed to conspire against the world's first and only unsinkable ship. On the night of April 14, some 400 miles east of the Newfoundland coast, the 882-foot (267 m) long liner side-swiped a massive iceberg. A 300-foot (91 m) gash was ripped in her side. The cut was fatal, the ship doomed. Within three hours, flooding steadily by the bow, her stern section lifted out of the water and she plunged to the bottom of 12,000-feet (3,600 m) of chilled north Atlantic water. It was the worst maritime tragedy ever.

The captain was lost, as were most of the steerage passengers, those terrified souls who were left in the labyrinth of their lower deck quarters and passageways. Those who found their way to the first-class section were often barred and so missed the chance to board the ship's few lifeboats. An estimated 1,522 people perished. Only 705 survived, approximately 32 percent of all those aboard the 46,300-ton (41,670 t) liner. The first rescue ship, a small Cunarder named *Carpathia,* arrived by dawn and began receiving the first lifeboats full of survivors, most of which were first-class passengers.

Only 32% of all those onboard the *Titanic* survived the voyage. Even when survivors landed at New York, many could not quite believe that she had sunk. The world's first "unsinkable" ship was gone, having never reached her destination. Underwater, the *Titanic* has broken in two and disintegrated substantially. The *Empress of Ireland* (opposite page), which sank two years later, remains in very good condition—she is in a freshwater grave in the St. Lawrence River.

The White Star Line never fully recovered from the *Titanic* sinking. Almost immediately, lifesaving regulations were extended and improved, and many ships, including *Olympic*, were given additional lifeboats. The general public deserved and demanded to be reassured. Certainly, there had to be far greater guarantees for safe passages on the North Atlantic.

Three years earlier, in January, 1909, another White Star liner was involved in an historic, but far less memorable, disaster. The 15,000-ton (13,500 t) *Republic* was in waters near New

York, off the Nantucket Lightship, when she collided with another passenger ship, the Italian *Florida*. The *Republic*, carrying over 2,000 passengers and crew, was badly damaged and in need of urgent assistance. From her bridge came the first SOS radio distress message in the history of sea travel. Rescue ships responded quickly and all but four of her passengers and crew were saved. This new distress system was soon used by all ships throughout the world. The tragedy was, however, fatal to the 585-foot (175 m) *Republic*. On the following day, some freighters attempted to tow the now empty ship to safety, but the damage was far too severe. She sank the day after the collision and so remains, in greatly deteriorated condition, on the ocean floor to this day. A nearby neighbor is the Italian liner *Andrea Doria*, which sank nearly half a century later.

The unfortunate captain of the doomed *Titanic*.

Britain suffered another horrific loss just two years after the *Titanic*, in May, 1914. Canadian Pacific's 14,000-ton (12,600 t) *Empress of Ireland* was among the largest and finest passenger ships then on the St. Lawrence River run, trading between Liverpool and Quebec City.

R.M.S. "EMPRESS of IRELAND"

FASTEST & FINEST to CANADA

570 feet in length, 65 feet broad, 14,500 tons, she has reciprocating engines of 18,500 horsepower and twin screws her shortest passage from land to land is 3 days 17 hours and 54 minutes, which constitutes the record from America to Europe. Her record days run westward is 469 and eastward 442.

While in the river, near Father Point, she was rammed in a very thick fog by a poorly navigated Norwegian freighter. The mortally wounded liner sank almost immediately and 1,024 perished. Britian's streak of bad luck did not end there: the nation would soon suffer another ocean liner loss, this one a wartime tragedy.

The sinking of Cunard's splendid 31,500-ton (28,350 t) *Lusitania* is surely the most famous sea tragedy of the First World War. Unlike her near sister, the speedy *Mauretania*, which was hurriedly converted for war duties, the *Lusitania* was kept in something of a neutral commercial service, sailing regularly between New York and Liverpool. She carried fare-paying passengers and commercial cargo, but some space was actually reserved for American war materials bound for Britain. And so, in May, 1915, with the official freight manifest including the likes of copper, cheese, and barrels of oysters, there was also far more ominous, more mysterious cargo in the ship's holds: shrapnel shells, cases of fuses, as well as 10 tons of explosives, six million rounds of ammunition, and hundreds of bales of so-called "raw furs," a volatile type of gun cotton that exploded when brought into contact with water.

It was believed that the "neutral" *Lusitania* was beyond attack. Simply, she was said to be too fast for the sinister German U-boats. However, just after lunch on May 7, a torpedo was fired from a German U-boat that pierced the 787-foot (236 m) long liner just under the starboard bridge wing. A thick column of steam and water spouted nearly 200 feet (60 m) in the air. With it went pieces of coal and wood and steel splinters. The *Lusitania* began to flood and took on a very serious list almost immediately. Then, quite suddenly, there was a tremendous second blast that ripped apart the bow section. Many survivors maintained that it was not a second torpedo or even a boiler explosion, but that mysterious wartime cargo in the forward hatches. The *Lusitania* sank within 18 minutes and plunged to the bottom of the sea off the southeastern coast of Ireland. An estimated 1,198 perished, of which 758 were passengers. However, one crew member, with exceptional luck, survived. Miraculously, this same man had also survived the sinking of the *Titanic* in 1912 and the *Empress of Ireland* in 1914!

The tragic sinking of the *Lusitania* was the third big British liner loss within three years. Reputed not to be carrying war supplies or ammunition, her attack in "peacetime" guise inspired American sympathy to what was then the British war against the Germans.

The mighty French liner *L'Atlantique* was a first cousin of sorts to the splendid *Ile de France*. They were both large, powerful, and exquisitely appointed, but they were built for different trades. While the *Ile* served New York on the North Atlantic run, the 42,500-ton (38,250 t) *L'Atlantique* was the largest liner yet built for the South Atlantic—for the run from Bordeaux to Rio and Buenos Aires. Tragically, she survived for only two years. On January 5, 1933, she burned out in the English Channel.

Fortunately, the *L'Atlantique* was empty at the time, with a reduced number of her crew on board. She was on a short "positioning trip," going from Bordeaux to drydocking in Le Havre, when the blaze erupted. The fire started in an empty first-class stateroom, spread quickly (particularly through the ship's electrical system) and then soon engulfed almost all of the liner's 742-foot (223 m) hull. Soon she was burning end to end and was abandoned. Several days passed before the liner, listing and badly blistered, could be reboarded. Examinations proved that she was a total loss, beyond any economically reasonable repair. She was, however, kept at Cherbourg for three years, a blackened wreck, mostly for the benefit of the under-

writers, who were battling over claims. Her owner, the Compagnie Sud-Atlantique, was finally

awarded $6.8 million in damages. The ship's remains were then sold to scrappers and, in deliv-

ery to the breakers at Glasgow, the corpselike wreckage of the once glorious *L'Atlantique* was

towed past the outbound, sparkling new *Queen Mary*.

One of the most mysterious of all passenger ship tragedies occurred aboard one of the

safest vessels of her time, the 11,500-ton (10,350 t) American cruise ship *Morro Castle*. On Sep-

tember 8, 1934, northbound from Havana to New York, the liner caught

fire while steaming off the New Jersey coast. Oddly, and despite some

very sophisticated fire detection equipment, the fires (there were sev-

eral) evidently had been smoldering for some time even prior to detec-

tion. A series of unexplainable further complications followed. The first

alarms were delayed by as much as 15 minutes, by which point the

flames had spread throughout the ship.

> *The* 19,000-ton Bermuda *was also quite unfortunate. Owned by Britain's Furness Bermuda Line, she was just three years old when, in June 1931, she was seriously damaged by fire at her Hamilton, Bermuda berth. Her owners felt, however, that costly repairs were warranted. She crossed the Atlantic to her builders' yard for repairs at Belfast, only to have a second, more serious fire erupt there. This time, she was finished. She even sank at her pier. Incredibly, there were more problems still. Once salvaged and sold off, she ran aground en route to the scrappers in Scotland.*

There was no reduction in the ship's speed and so the wind fanned

the blaze even further. The distress calls were not sent until the 531-foot (159 m) *Morro Castle*

was a torch; other nearby ships had already reported the fire. By this time, there was chaos

among the 555 passengers and crew on board. Only six lifeboats were lowered and these were

filled mostly with crew rather than passengers. When the rescue ships finally arrived, it was

too late for many—in all, 133 perished. Even an attempt to tow the liner failed when the hawser

lines broke. Later, the ship itself, still afire, drifted ashore on the beach of Asbury Park. What a

frightening, grotesque sight she made to the thousands who journeyed especially to see her.

Beyond repair, she was later towed away and then scrapped.

Fire also proved to be the ending for that most exquisite of superliners, the French

Normandie. When the war in Europe started, she was laid up at New York's Pier 88, in Septem-

ber, 1939. Sadly, she would never sail again. She might have become a high-capacity military

troopship, like those other giants, the *Queen Mary* and *Queen Elizabeth*, and was seized by the

U.S. government in December, 1941 for this purpose. She was renamed U.S.S. *Lafayette* and

was in the process of being hurriedly stripped and converted when, the following February 9,

The Paris *had been loaded with national treasures bound for the World's Fair at New York when she caught fire at the Le Havre dockside. The fire sent clouds of black smoke out over the city. Firefighters poured so much water onto the blazing ship that she capsized.*

a fire erupted. Sparks from a workman's acetylene torch ignited a pile of kapok lifejackets and triggered the blaze. The ship was evacuated as the fire spread. Huge clouds of orange-brown smoke covered midtown Manhattan as the 83,400-ton (75,060 t) *Normandie* burned to death.

Maddening excitement led to miscalculation. Overzealous firefighters continuously and haphazardly poured tons of water onto the burning 1028-foot (308 m) long liner. The weight was too much. In the early hours of the next day, she capsized—lying on her side, like a beached whale, at the foot of West 48th Street, in New York City's backyard. In this position, she presented the most difficult salvage task of all time. All of her upper works—the masts and funnels and the decking—had to be removed as pumps simultaneously pushed water out of her vast hull. It took over 15 months to do the job and cost a staggering $5 million. The disaster had one redeeming factor, however: the *Normandie* was used as a wartime U.S. navy diving school.

A similar but even more pathetic fate awaited the magnificent *Normandie*. When she caught fire on a cold afternoon in February 1942, while at her New York berth, firefighters were again far too zealous, and so overloaded her with tons of water that she capsized as well. Later, she had to be partially dismantled, pumped out, then righted and finally towed off to a local scrapyard.

The remains of the *Normandie* were laid up for several years, a wrecked hulk, and although there were rumors that she might be rebuilt as an aircraft carrier or as a medium-sized liner, she was finally declared surplus in 1945. A year later, she was sold for scrap to a local firm in New York harbor. In the end, her remains fetched a pathetic $161,000.

Two of the very worst, but largely forgotten tragedies at sea represent the extraordinary loss of over 10,000 lives. Both involved otherwise splendid German passenger ships. The 25,000-ton (22,860 t) *Wilhelm Gustloff* was built by the Nazi regime in 1938, as a special cruise ship for party members and their families. Mostly, her passengers were workers, and their inex-

pensively priced trips were coupled with on board political indoctrination sessions. She had barely seen service, however, when, in September, 1939, she was called to war duties—first as a hospital ship and then as a floating barracks. Tragically, and shortly before the collapse of Nazi Germany, she was used, in January, 1945, to evacuate refugees and soldiers from the so-called Eastern territories. Overloaded with an estimated 6,100 on board, she was escaping to a German port when she was attacked by a Soviet submarine and hit with three torpedoes. She quickly capsized and all but 904 people were lost. Over 5,200 refugees, prisoners, hospital patients, soldiers, and crewmembers died. Some reports even suggest, and primarily because of uncertain record keeping at the time, that there were actually 5,400 losses. Undoubtedly, it remains the worst sea loss ever.

The *Cap Arcona* was also lost with mind-boggling casualties in those final dark days of the Second World War. At 27,600 tons (24,400 t) she was the flagship of the Hamburg South America Line fleet, the German queen of the Latin American run to Rio and Buenos Aires. First used as a barracks ship during the war, she began evacuation sailings in early 1945. Months later, on May 3, after several successful trips and only days away from the Nazi surrender, she was attacked by British bombers, who were unaware that 6,000 people were on board. She was quickly afire and soon capsized. Over 5,000 perished.

The *Andrea Doria* **was the tour de force of post-second World War Italian ocean-going splendor. Her loss in July 1956, when she was only three years old, was a tremendous blow. The Swedish ship that rammed and sank her, the** *Stockholm*, **was referred to as "the villain." Even many years later, in 1989, when the former** *Stockholm* **appeared in Genoa, the** *Doria*'s **homeport, local newspapers referred to her as the "death ship."**

The most newsworthy liner disaster following the Second World War involved the new flagship of Italy's rebuilt liner fleet, the 700-foot (201 m) long *Andrea Doria*. In the crowded North Atlantic sea-lanes, this was the worst collision between two passenger ships. Sweden's little 12,600-ton (113,400 t) *Stockholm*, outbound from New York, fatally rammed the 29,000-ton (26,100 t) Italian ship in the fog-shrouded waters off Nantucket. The *Doria* was wounded just below the starboard bridge and though considered to be one of the safest ships afloat at that time (that word "unsinkable" was again put to use), she was doomed. She sank in the early morning of the following day, July 26, 1956. Minus her bow, the *Stockholm* limped back to New York and then to shipyard repairs. In all, 52 lives were lost. The court inquiries that followed, which were held in the tightest secrecy, never established the actual blame. The full settlements amounted to $48 million. The Italians remained bitter and the Swedes denied responsibility.

In happier days, in the twenties and thirties, the *Cap Arcona* was the German queen of the South American route. She was large, fast, and notably lavish and luxurious. But her ending was one of the worst of all—as many as 5,400 casualties occurred when she was torpedoed in that fateful spring of 1945.

The *Doria*, resting on her side, soon became a nesting for sea life and a mass of tangled fishing nets. She initially was the subject of considerable speculation on possible salvage. There were all sorts of schemes, including dragging her to the surface with heavy-duty chains and even filling her with ping-pong balls for flotation. One entrepeneur, full of wild enthusiasm, envisioned raising the liner, then towing her into New York harbor and finally cutting up her remains for resale as cufflinks and tie clips. However, none of these schemes came to pass, and the *Andrea Doria* still lies on the bottom of the ocean, home to marine life.

CRUISES: VOYAGES TO THE SUN

CRUISING IS A TYPE OF TRAVEL QUITE DIFFERENT FROM THE VOYAGES PREVIOUSLY

described in these pages. A cruise is more of a purely recreational voyage. It is a sailing without

a destination, in which the ports instead are diversions—indeed, port calls are simply daily

activities. The older liners on the transatlantic runs moved passengers, be it in the splendid

opulence of first class or in the cramped bowels of steerage, from one place to another destina-

tion. The primary goal of such liners was the movement of people. But today, cruising is the

absolute, almost complete mainstay of the international ocean liner business. Even the *Queen*

Elizabeth 2, which still offers the transatlantic crossings, is run more like a cruise ship than one

of those traditional, class-divided steamers of the past. Today it is mostly aircraft that move

travelers from point A to point B.

The very first cruise was said to have been offered to the public in 1857. It was a sightseeing

The first liners built for full-time cruising did not appear until after the Second World War. By the 1950s, cruises to warm and sunny climes were becoming increasingly popular and affordable.

voyage of sorts to the antiquities of the then rather remote Mediterranean. A British ship, the *Ceylon*, owned by the illustriously historic P&O Company, was used for the voyage. It was all rather primitive, long before air-conditioned staterooms, lido decks with oval-shaped pools, and even the luxury of comfortable tour buses onshore to ferry the passengers to all those temples and treasures. Indeed, the *Ceylon*'s passengers were adventurers, filled with the spirit of exploring, and certainly well-heeled. Earlier, in 1835, an advertisement was run in an Edinburgh newspaper for "tourists," and proposing a "cruise" to the very remote Faroe Islands north of Scotland and onwards even to Iceland. It was far too adventurous for most people of the time and the voyage never quite set off.

Following the *Ceylon*'s inaugural pleasure jaunt, cruises remained rather intermittent. They were daring journeys, still restricted primarily to the more adventurous souls or, as one advertisement called them, "the educational and scientific oriented travelers." But by the twilight of the Victorian Age, in the 1890s, there were increasing numbers of people who had both the spare time and the funds to make these "voyages of recreation and rest." Germany's Hamburg America Line, already one of the world's mightiest shippers, was interested in pursuing this market and so dispatched some of their smaller ships to the West Indies, the Mediterranean, Scandinavia, and, on occasion, to such exotic destinations as Egypt, Spitzbergen, and West Africa. Quaintly, the eastern Mediterranean was still referred to as the Orient. In Britian, the well-known Orient Line, which normally ran its passenger ships on line voyages to Australia, began to offer leisure cruises, also to the Mediterranean and Scandinavia.

It was Hamburg America that, with considerable foresight and courage, built the world's first cruise ship. She was the *Prinzessin Victoria Luise* of 1900. Although she was only 4,400 tons (3,960 t) and 407 feet (122 m) in length, her small size was a deliberate decision: she was planned to resemble the royal yachts of Europe and to attract a specific clientele. Her passengers were to be only the very rich, travelers who could spend weeks on board and who wanted the very finest in service. The Kaiser himself inspected the ship, and was quite dismayed to discover that she was actually larger than his own imperial yacht. Hamburg America directors were, however, thoughtful in planning a special royal suite on board and would happily make available their new cruising ship to His Majesty. His sense of dismay was thus appeased. In addition, there were 119 other staterooms on board, which could altogether berth

The world's first specially-built cruiseship was Hamburg America Line's *Prinzessin Victoria Luise*. She was designed to be a luxurious ship, deliberately fashioned after the royal yachts of Europe. Her ornate accommodations were reminders of the first class quarters on the big transatlantic express liners.

nearly 400 passengers. For the first time aboard any commercial passenger vessel, every room had a complete bedroom, private drawing room, and full bathroom. Sadly, however, life for the world's first cruise ship was all too brief. Within six years, by 1906, she went aground on Jamaica during a Caribbean trip and was a complete wreck.

The Hamburg America Line continued its interest in cruises, however, and even carried members of the German imperial family as guests. The future of cruising seemed bright, and more and more cruise sailings were on the boards. When the sisters *Cleveland* and *Cincinnati* were built in 1909, they were novel in being built not only for regular, class-divided North Atlantic sailings, but also for cruising. Beginning in January, 1910, the *Cleveland* offered wintertime circumnavigations of the globe, extraordinary 110-day trips that were booked by as many as 650 tourists. In short time, both sisters were running these off-season voyages. The fares ranged from $6,600 for a top suite, with bedroom and bath, to smaller third-class cabins on "F Deck" that were sold to "gentlemen only" for $650.

At about the same time, Hamburg America committed itself further to investing in cruising. Their large and mighty transatlantic Blue Ribbon champion, the 16,700-ton (15,030 t) *Deutschland*, had been consistently troublesome, mostly with her mechanics, and so she was brought in for conversion in 1910–11. She was repainted in all-white and her original berthing of 2,050 in four classes reduced drastically to 487, all first class. Thus, the *Deutschland* not only became the world's largest cruise ship, but the most spacious as well. She was even renamed, becoming the *Victoria Luise*, surely a case of early marketing considering the similarity in name to that earlier, highly acclaimed cruising yacht, the *Prinzessin Victoria Luise*. The larger ship, with her extravagant salons and first-class suites, a grill room, and even a full gymnasium and a canvas swimming pool on deck, roamed through the West Indian islands, the ports of the Mediterranean, and the Norwegian fjords. On occasion, because of her noted luxuries, she even acted as a "host ship" for the Imperial German aristocracy for such events as naval reviews and official regattas.

After the First World War, cruising resumed at even greater pace, but mostly on longer, more expensive trips. Cruising had still not come to the masses. Now, even the world's largest

The decor of the very early cruising ships was meant to remind passengers of home. A single berth cabin circa 1890 is shown below.

liners, such as Cunard's speedy *Mauretania* and the splendid *Aquitania*, sought employment off the cold, dreary, and often ferocious North Atlantic. There were fewer transoceanic passengers about and so these ships were temporarily made into all first-class resort-floating hotels and sent off on Caribbean and Mediterranean itineraries. The *Mauretania* might travel for six weeks, calling in at such ports as Madeira, Naples, and Villefranche on the famed French Riviera, in the absolute lap of seagoing luxury: 200 or so millionaires being looked after by 800 or so crew members. If passage rates seemed lower, at a rather scant $600, then the cost of labor was far less. The economic picture, the business of running passenger liners, was far different.

The first official around-the-world cruise, all first class and catering purely to the monied set, was run in the winter of 1922, by the 18,000-ton (20,000 t) Cunarder *Laconia*. It was an instant success and soon not only other Cunard liners, but other noted passenger ships followed in the *Laconia*'s wake. Red Star Line's *Belgenland*, a prestigious Atlantic liner, capped by three funnels, weighing nearly 25,000 tons and with space for over 2,500 passengers, soon established herself as a favorite. Her annual sailings became something of a tradition, particularly in the late twenties. An advertisement for her 1925–26 world cruise read:

Cruising in European waters increased considerably in the 1930s, providing escape from the gloom of the Depression. There were popular trips to Spain and Portugal, the Canaries, West Africa, the Mediterranean, and Scandinavia. Short two- to five-day runs to ports like Amsterdam and Hamburg, and to the Scottish Isles, were also popular.

BELGENLAND WORLD CRUISE

Largest and finest liner ever to circle the globe. You will enjoy the courtesies accorded this outstanding world cruiser whose passengers are received as visitors of note. You will appreciate the timeliness of the sailing and the skillful arrangement of itinerary, which follows the sunshine and brings you to each of the 14 countries at its best travel season.

You will see, most pleasantly, what the wide world has to offer of beauty, of mystery, of contrast of culture and civilization, because of the perfectly arranged shore trips under the guidance of the American Express Company.

Sailing westward from New York, November 25, from Los Angeles on December 11, from San Francisco, December 14. Returning to New York on April 6, 1926. 132 days. 60 cities. 14 countries. Restricted to 475 passengers.

The itinerary was nothing short of spectacular: Havana, Balboa, the Panama Canal, Los Angeles, San Francisco, Hilo, Honolulu, Yokohama, Tokyo, Nikko, Kamakura, Kobe, Nara, Kyoto, the Inland Sea, Shanghai, Hong Kong, Macao, Manila, Batavia, Singapore, Diamond Harbor, Calcutta, Kandy, Colombo, Bombay, Port Sudan, Port Tewfik, Cairo, Alexandria, Naples, Monaco, Nice, and Gibraltar.

There were, of course, other long-distance cruises, such as the Great Africa cruise of 1926.

THE GREAT AFRICA CRUISE

Sailing from New York, January 19, 1926, on the palatial cruising liner *Orca* to the West Indies: Trinidad. South America: Rio de Janeiro, Santos, Montevideo, and Buenos Aires. South Africa: Capetown, Port Elizabeth, and Durban. East Africa: Delagoa Bay, Beira, Mozambique, Zanzibar, and Mombasa. Egypt: Port Sudan, the Nile, Cairo, and Alexandria. The Mediterranean and Europe: Naples, the Riviera, Gibraltar, and Southampton.

The lure of Africa! You will have three weeks in gorgeous South Africa and on the wondrous East African Coast. But first—through the West Indies—to those magnificent cities of South America—across the South Atlantic.

After Africa—Egypt—favorite Mediterranean and European places. Delightful shore excursions in all countries visited. Optional tours to Victoria Falls, Khartoum, Luxor, the Holy Land, and other interesting places.

This is the "cruise you have been waiting for"—22,500 miles—20 ports—100 glorious days. Rates, incuding shore excursions, from $1,250. "The Comfort Route"—The Royal Mail Steam Packet Company.

It was still the world cruise that remained the byword in luxurious ocean travel, however. Passengers went year after year, and often brought along their own servants and even requested, for a cozy sense of familiarity, the same stateroom. To some, it was much like a large, floating country club. The *Belgenland*'s premier reputation for circumnavigations was passed on to the likes of Cunard's *Carinthia* and *Franconia*, and perhaps even more so the superb *Empress of Britain*, that extraordinary 42,000 tonner (378,000 t), the largest ever built for the Atlantic trade to Eastern Canada, but with her accommodations almost halved to only 700. The

M ____
Str. ____
Stateroom ____
HONOLULU

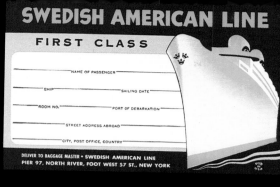

SWEDISH AMERICAN LINE
FIRST CLASS

NAME OF PASSENGER
SHIP ____ SAILING DATE ____
ROOM NO. ____ PORT OF DEBARKATION ____
STREET ADDRESS ABROAD ____
CITY, POST OFFICE, COUNTRY ____

DELIVER TO BAGGAGE MASTER · SWEDISH AMERICAN LINE
PIER 97, NORTH RIVER, FOOT WEST 57 ST., NEW YORK

MESSAGERIES MARITIMES
NOM
PAQUEBOT
DATE de DÉPART
DESTINATION
CALE
SANS ACCÈS PENDANT LE VOYAGE

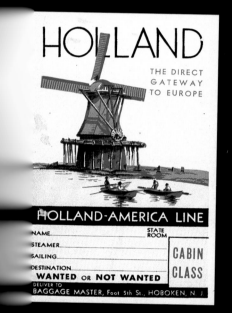

HOLLAND
THE DIRECT GATEWAY TO EUROPE

HOLLAND-AMERICA LINE
NAME ____ STATE ROOM ____
STEAMER ____
SAILING ____ **CABIN CLASS**
DESTINATION ____
WANTED or NOT WANTED
DELIVER TO
BAGGAGE MASTER, Foot 5th St., HOBOKEN, N. J

NIPPON YUSEN KAISHA
Destination
M ____
Cabin No. ____ Berth ____
SS ____
NOT WANTED
PRINTED IN JAPAN

STATE ROOM
DOLLAR
STEAMSHIP LINES
BAGGAGE ROOM
M ____
S. S. PRESIDENT ____ PIER ____
CABIN ____ TO ____

"ITALIA" NAVIGAZIONE
CRISTOFORO COLOMBO
" ITALIAN LINE "

CUNARD LINE to E
AQUITANIA
NAME ____
SHIP ____ SAILING ____
FROM ____ TO ____
CLASS ____ STATEROOM NUMBER or HOLD ____

LIBERTÉ
Cie TRANSATLANTIQUE French Line
PASSENGER'S NAME ____
SAILING ____ CABIN ____
FINAL DESTINATION ____
PRINTED IN FRANCE

French Line
PIER 57 NORTH RIVER
PIER 90 NORTH RIVER
NEW YORK

CUNARD LINE CRUISES
SHIP ____
NAME ____
STATEROOM ____
PRINTED IN ENGLAND

CUNARD WHITE STAR
QUEEN MARY
TO EUROPE

CANADIAN PACIFIC
1
NAME ____
TO ____
S.S. ____
SAILING ____ ROOM Nº ____
FINAL DESTINATION ____
1
NOT WANTED

service, space, and overall comfort ratios were exceptional. She might well have been classed as the world's biggest yacht. She too went round the world each winter, and the advance promotions for her 1936 cruise read:

WAKE UP SOME MORNING IN BALI

How would you like to wake up some morning next winter in your own luxurious apartment, complete with every facility for comfortable living . . . then step out on the shores of incredible Bali, last exotic stand of simple nature?

Then cruise on to new thrills, new adventures? And between strange ports, amuse yourself with real tennis on a full-size court, swimming in a spacious pool, and the varied entertainments that can be offered only on a ship like the *Empress of Britain* . . . the largest liner that ever went around the world.

This is exactly the way this cruise takes you to eight Mediterranean cities, through Egypt and India, via the Malacca Straits to Siam, Cambodia, and Java . . . up into China and Japan . . . and home by way of Hawaii, the Panama Canal, and the West Indies.

Cruise sails from New York, January 9, 130 days. 31 ports. Fares from $2,150. Apartments with bath from $3,800. Both include standard shore excursion program. P.S. For a shorter cruise, take the Africa–South America Cruise. 23 ports. 95 days. *Empress of Australia*. From New York January 25. Fares from $1,350 (rooms with bath $2,350), including standard shore program.

Ocean cruising did, in fact, come to the masses during the otherwise hard-pressed, Depression-era thirties. There were short runs to Bermuda, Nassau, and Havana, and even on northern routes, to Halifax and Boston. Cheapest of all were the overnight "cruises to nowhere," parties at sea with the bars open, despite the rigors of Prohibition. They were priced

Holland's Rotterdam Lloyd was one of the more exotic firms. Their big, grey-hulled passenger liners plied the Eastern route—out through the Mediterranean and the Suez, along the Red Sea and into the Indian Ocean, and finally to colonial Java. Onboard were colonial high commissioners, tea and rubber planters, commercial merchants, teachers, missionaries, and nurses.

from $10 and often were scheduled on such illustrious liners as the *Mauretania*, the *Berengaria*, and the *Majestic*. From these "booze cruises," as they were also known, thousands began to graduate, if you will, to longer sailings: four, five, and seven days and then to as much as two weeks.

Two notable ships of the time were the *Monarch of Bermuda* and the *Queen of Bermuda* of Britain's Furness Bermuda Line. Introduced in 1931 and 1933 respectively, and weighing over 22,500 tons (20,250 t) they were as luxurious as any North Atlantic liner, featured private facilities in every cabin, and ran $50 six-day cruises between New York and beautiful Bermuda. They became known as the "millionaire ships," high-quality liners for inexpensive fares. Because of their Saturday afternoon departures from New York, they also became favorites of the just-married set and so earned another nickname—"the honeymoon ships." Thereafter, more and more liners would be planned for shorter cruises and for the enjoyment of the rapidly increasing numbers of more middle income sea travelers. If only millionaires could afford the *Empress of Britain*'s world cruises, a new generation of clerks, secretaries, and schoolteachers could at least afford a five-day trip to Nassau aboard the same ship.

Today in the booming North American cruise industry, there is a vast selection of cruise offerings: voyages to the tropics, with shimmering waters and moonlit nights; to well-known and remote ports; on big liners or smaller, yacht-like ships. There is something to suit every taste—and pocketbook. One might think such a wide selection of cruises is a recent development, but, 50 years ago, even as the Depression lingered and the world teetered on the threshold of another global conflict, there were many cruise sailings in the winter of 1938–39. Sailing mostly from New York in those days (a rarity in these times, as Miami has long since replaced that northern port as the ocean liner capital), there were such quick trips as four days over Christmas to Bermuda for $43 aboard one of the most luxurious liners of all time, Canadian Pacific's sumptuous *Empress of Britain*. Alternately, in the short cruise range, there was United States Lines' *Manhattan* for six days to Havana from $75, and Anchor Line's *Transylvania* for

*E*ven the most illustrious North Atlantic liners went cruising in the otherwise hard-pressed early thirties. The transatlantic trade had slumped so badly in those Depression years that low-fare cruises out of New York, Southampton and Liverpool seemed the best alternative. Legendary ships like the Berengaria were sent on short runs to Bermuda, Nassau, and even on "weekends to nowhere." There were one-nighters out past the three-mile limits—so-called "booze cruises." Those who remembered the Berengaria in palmier days now dubbed her the "Bargain-area."

COMPAGNIE GÉNÉRALE TRANSATLANTIQUE
French Line

eight days to Nassau and Havana, from $80. Eleven days to the Caribbean in the French *Champlain* cost $140 and 15 days on the Swedish *Kungsholm* started at $182.50.

Longer cruises were still very popular and, in a three-month period from December, 1938 through March, there were 15 sailings of 24 days and longer. There were three South American trips, all of which put into fabled Rio. Two of these were aboard some of the greatest and grandest dream boats ever, both floating temples of the age of Art Deco: France's flawlessly magnificent *Normandie* (24 days, starting at $435) and Holland's brand new *Nieuw Amsterdam* (25 days, $360). There were three other trips to South America, but these were longer and went completely around the continent. One of the largest and fastest of all Atlantic liners, North German Lloyd's 51,000 ton (45,900 t) *Bremen*, made the trip in 40 days with fares from $725. Yet the ultimate cruises were trips around the world. All three set sail in January within two weeks of one another: Cunard's *Franconia* for 147 days, at $1,900; the *Empress of Britain*, 128 days, $2,300 and the Norwegian cruising yacht *Stella Polaris* for 111 days from $1,250.

Now, it all seems so fascinating, so intriguing, and so affordable: $18 a day to Rio aboard the exquisite *Normandie*. All aboard!

THE WORLD'S LARGEST SHIP

SHIPS

OF

TODAY &

BEYOND

THE FIRST BIG LINER TO BE BUILT SPECIFICALLY FOR FULL-TIME CRUISING APPEARED

just after the Second World War. She was Cunard's renowned *Caronia* of 1948. She reflected a

grander, more comfortable, and certainly less cost-conscious era. She also reflected those ear-

lier winter cruise ships, the ones that made the fabled long-distance cruises around the world,

around continental Africa, and through the entire Mediterranean. At 34,000 tons (30,600 t) and

715 feet (214 m) in length, she was a large liner, as large as many national flagships (the flagship

of the entire U.S. fleet, the 33,500-ton (30,150 t) *America* comes to mind), and her approxi-

mately 600 cruise passengers would be looked after by an equal number of staff. Internally, she

had the spacious, clubby, stuffed-chair-with-pillows feel that was so typical of British liners and

particularly of Cunarders. Her owners wanted her to be distinctive, however, and so, to the

surprise of many on her delivery, she was painted overall in four shades of green. The plan

The *Fair Princess*
carries passengers on
trips that range from
Caribbean cruises to
Alaskan jaunts.

worked. In no time at all, the *Caronia* was dubbed the "green goddess." Everything about her was luxurious in scale—from her restaurant menus to her handpicked staff to the private bathroom facilities in all of her cabins.

The *Caronia* quickly became something of a floating clubhouse. Several passengers lived on board for years, others took many trips in succession. Her operations had a prescribed formula: in January, she left New York for a three-month trip around the world (or around the Pacific or continental Africa); in spring, she went to the Mediterranean for as long as eight weeks; in summer, her destination was Scandinavia for six weeks; and finally, two more Mediterranean runs in the autumn before annual drydocking and a return to New York to repeat the formula. For over a decade, she was queen of all cruise ships, the pacesetter, the standard by which others were judged. The age of the specifically designed cruise ship had arrived, as the magnificent era of the big, class-divided transatlantic giants was nearing its end. The jet had arrived and proved unbeatable, and so even the veteran *Queen Mary*, in something of a last ditch effort, was sent off on sunshine runs to Nassau— five days for $125 in 1963. Yet these ships, the *Queens,* the *United States,*

The *Caronia*, the first big liner built specifically for cruising, had a country club atmosphere. Some passengers travelled in her year after year, others for several trips at a time, and still others, although a far more select group, lived onboard for two or three years in succession. One woman broke all records, however. She sailed the *Caronia* for fourteen years.

and finally even the *Caronia,* were out of step with the times. A new, more modern, far flashier breed of cruise ship was on the boards. It was the age of the wedding cake cruise ship: all white, higher and higher, raked and streamlined, and gradually looking less and less like those classic liners of yesteryear. The funnel gradually changed, as well: some now house cocktail lounges, others look like airplane tails, and still others are virtually nonexistent.

The 39,200-ton (35,280 t) *Oceanic,* completed in 1965 by the Italians and owned by the Swiss-based, Panama-registered Home Lines, was one of the great turning points in ocean liner design and thinking. Although she was originally intended for two-class North-Atlantic service on the St. Lawrence, her owners re-evaluated her prospects soon after launching. They decided to use this large and luxurious new breed of liner, in year-round cruise service out of New York. Never before had a ship of this size (1,600 maximum berths) been used for full-time cruising.

Previously, the only year-round cruise ships out of New York were of vintage stock: the *Nassau*,

a former P&O Australian liner from the early twenties, and the *Italia*, also of the Home Lines,

and the ex-Swedish *Kungsholm* of 1928. The *Oceanic*'s cruises, priced for $170 beginning in

April, 1965, were an instant success. More full-time cruise ships followed. Cunard's *Franconia*

was taken off the Montreal run and sent on weekly sunshine runs to Bermuda in 1967 and the

The Oceanic (above) was a trend-setting cruiseship for the 1960s. Not only was her funnel placed aft, therefore creating more deck space, but her twin center pools were covered by a retractable glass dome. The *Rotterdam* (right) was one of the great transitions, changed from a two-class Atlantic liner to a one-class cruiseship. Her ports of call now include Alaska's Glacier Bay, Curacao, and Nassau.

transatlantic *Rotterdam* was made into an all first-class cruise ship in 1969.

A year after the *Oceanic*'s debut at New York, a much smaller, but equally significant cruise ship came into service. She was the Norwegian *Sunward* of 1966. She was the first high-standard, luxury vessel to cruise out of Miami, a port that had been previously served by a few overaged, well-used passenger ships. The 11,000-ton (9,900 t) *Sunward* had actually been built for the England–Spain tourist run, but almost from the start there were serious complications, mostly arriving from the British Government's tourist restrictions. Consequently, her Oslo-based owners looked elsewhere and saw promise in a year-round Miami cruise service. An Israeli car ferry had been in use there, but she was recalled by her owners, so there was an opening for the 558-passenger *Sunward*. Success was instant and overwhelming. That first smallish ship was in service barely a year when two larger, better equipped sister ships were ordered. The owners styled themselves the Norwegian Caribbean Lines and even moved their operational base to Miami. Other Norwegian shipowners, even those who had no background

in passenger shipping, saw a bright future in Florida cruising. The next creation was the Royal Caribbean Cruise Lines.

While the *Oceanic* and several other cruise ships remained quite successful for some years sailing out of New York, Miami gradually became the most important cruise center in the world. Clearly, it was the geography, its very closeness to the Bahamas that made Miami the perfect port for increasingly popular three- and four-day trips. It was also convenient for trips to the Caribbean islands, mostly for seven-day sailings, but also 10–14-day runs. Passengers, especially first-timers, wanted as much warm weather and smooth sailing time as possible, and the opportunity to sample more ports. Those island stopovers became cherished souvenirs. Years later, by the 1980s, San Juan, Puerto Rico would grow enormously as a cruise departure port because of its even closer proximity to other islands—ships could visit six ports in seven days! New York, of course, lost its preeminence when the Atlantic liners faded away and cruise passengers realized that they often had to endure several expensive and often uncomfortable

R.M.S
QUEEN MARY

HOLLAND·AMERIKA LIJN

ROTTERDAM·NEW YORK
VIA BOULOGNE SUR MER

The Blue Funnel Line

S.S.
DEMOSTHENES

AMERICAN MAIL LINE

COMPAGNIE GENERALE TRANSATLANTIQUE

The Route
to the Riviera
and the
Mediterranean

FRENCH LINE   A.J.LEON. LITHO. N.Y.

Cie Gle TRANSATLANTIQUE
FRENCH LINE

SS « ROCHAMBEAU » (Pont-promenade).

N.Y.K. LINE M.S. "HEIAN MARU"

N.Y.K. LINE M.S. "HEIAN MARU"

sea days when traveling to and from the Caribbean. Today New York hosts only a dozen cruise ships a year (there were 60 passenger ships in regular service in the fifties) and these only part-time, from April to October. Their sailings are mostly to Bermuda or scenic runs to the St. Lawrence and New England. In winter, the Manhattan passenger terminal, three piers revitalized from the old transatlantic era, is used for exhibitions, private parties, and even weekend flea markets. Ironically, one of these specializes in vintage ocean liner memorabilia—china, menu cards, and baggage tags. Simultaneously, Miami handled over 35 different cruise liners, including those on special visits, and all of them in an exceptionally efficient series of terminals and docks, reception areas, and parking lots on the specially extended Dodge Island. On a Saturday afternoon, in the prime winter months, there might be as many as eight noted cruise ships, including the four largest passenger ships afloat, taking on 10–12,000 travelers. Few of them actually come from the Miami area, however. Some people come from Florida itself, but mostly these pleasure-seeking voyagers arrive by specially arranged air connections from almost all of the other 49 states.

By the early seventies, specialty cruise ships grew and grew, and simultaneously became more and more specialized. Royal Caribbean Cruise Lines' trio, beginning with the *Song of Norway* in 1970, followed by the twin sisters, *Nordic Prince* and *Sun Viking,* were among the finest ships of their day. Designed especially for the Miami–Caribbean trade (they would be fully booked for as long as the next 10 years!), the key element of their creation and operation was consistency. The ships were virtually identical, the food similar, and the entertainers shared and rotated among the three. This made for easier operation, especially for the crews, and also provided similarity and familiarity for passengers. There were growing numbers of those prized "repeaters," voyagers who wanted to sail again and again with the same company, but on a different cruise itinerary. It worked very well and Royal Caribbean Cruise Lines soon boasted a very impressive 30 percent repeat factor, one of the very highest in the cruise business. In general design, these ships were bright and colorful and inviting, with festive lounges,

Evocative postcards, metallic badges, and flags hint of far-away ports: the Holland America Line across the North Atlantic, the Blue Funnel Line out to the Far East, the French Line on Mediterranean cruises and the N.Y.K. Line of crossings to Japan. The badge with N.A.S.M. refers to Holland America, and another naming the steamer *Demosthenes* is of the Shaw Savill Line.

long bars, and spacious restaurants. There were also pools and saunas, outdoor buffet breakfasts and luncheons, discos and mini shopping centers, and, of course, the inevitable casinos, those increasingly popular blackjack and roulette arenas where passengers tried to reclaim at least some of their fares. Their most notable design distinction was, however, a cocktail lounge placed above the highest sun deck in the ship's funnel. While sipping a martini or a margarita before dinner, for example, passengers had the chance to witness a shimmering sunset.

Sometimes, cruise owners are cautious about the future growth of their markets. In the late seventies, the Royal Caribbean Cruise Lines, among others, wanted extra berths, but not completely new ships. Cleverly, they had their Song of Norway *and* Nordic Prince *cut in half and stretched—85-foot (26 m) midsections were inserted, increasing their capacities form 876 to 1,276.*

Another new Norwegian entry in what could be called the "cruising sweepstakes" was the Royal Viking Line. They too built three cruisers, a 21,000-ton (18,900 t) trio named *Royal Viking Star, Royal Viking Sky,* and *Royal Viking Sea.* Like several of their contemporaries, they also came from Finland, from the highly productive and ingenious Wartsila shipyard. In the seventies, this firm would become the master passenger shipbuilder, taking preeminence in a field long dominated by the British. Royal Viking was not, however, interested in short hops to Nassau or week-long runs to the lower Caribbean, but instead in long, luxurious, very expensive voyages, from two weeks to 100 days. These sparkling Vikings were the heiresses of sorts to the old *Belgenland* and *Empress of Britain.* They

128

would be acclaimed as among the very finest ships afloat. A legion of loyal followers included members of that old regime, "the *Caronia* set," who lived on board for months, if not several years, and others who took two or three voyages in succession. The planning was quite clever and thoughtful: passengers could often remain on board for as long as a year and not repeat the same itinerary. The sailings were listed in a lavish guidebook that was aptly called "the atlas." There were the expected trips to Scandinavia and the Baltic, but also sailings to the Mediterranean and the Black Sea, the Atlantic Isles and West Africa, and also more extensive and exotic voyages to the South Seas and lower South America, Southeast Asia, and the Indonesian islands. Naturally there was an annual circumnavigation, in the tradition of the *Caronia* and others, which was often booked a full year in advance. It seemed as though the luxury cruise business had a future as well.

At about the same time, in 1971–72, a Florida shipping agent named Ted Arison decided to form his own cruise line. He named it Carnival Cruise Lines because he wanted it, from the very first impression, to convey the fun image of cruising. A Carnival cruise was to be "the most relaxing vacation experience of all." Later, his fleet would even be known as the "fun ships." He too saw unlimited potential in the Miami–Caribbean market, but with two differ-

The white-hulled cruiseships of the Royal Caribbean Cruise Lines (Nordic Prince, left, and Sun Viking, above) have been among the most successful of all contemporary liners. It is said that everything about them is in just the right proportion. Among their most popular amenities are the cocktail lounges perched in their smokestacks.

ences. He felt that lower, more competitive pricing would lure even more first-timers and that

with sufficient cosmetic surgery, older, secondhand ships were quite adequate. And so, with a

very tight budget, he bought his first ship, Canadian Pacific's out-of-work flagship *Empress of*

Canada. She became the *Mardi Gras* and work crews joined her very first tropical sailings to

change the vessel from Atlantic liner to sunshine cruiser. They worked in restricted areas,

barely disturbing those otherwise happy guests. Arison was right on both counts and later

would become the most important figure in contemporary cruising. Carnival convinced more

travelers to take their first cruise than any other company. He bought two more secondhand

liners by 1978, and purchased his first brand-new ship, a 36,000-tonner (32,400 t) named *Tropi-*

cale, two years later. By the mid-1980s, he added three "mega-cruise ships," each of them big-

ger than the *Titanic,* to be followed beginning in 1990 by three more—these to be the among

the largest liners ever built, at 70,000 tons (63,000 t) each. Carnival became the biggest and

Carnival Cruise Lines, begun with a second-hand ship in 1972, was the world's largest and busiest cruise operator by 1990. In addition to ten ships of their own, they also have the four liners of Holland America Line and the three of Wind-star Sail Cruises. The *Jubilee*, commissioned in 1986, is one of their mega-cruisers at 47,000 tons and with capacity for 1,840 passengers.

busiest cruise company of all and in 1989 purchased the entire Holland America fleet and its subsidiaries, Windstar Sail Cruises, for cruising under "computer-operated" sails, and Wes-tours, the giant Alaska hotel and tour operator.

The general cruise forecast dimmed, however, in the mid-seventies. There were dramatic fuel oil increases that sent shipping managers shuddering (and some ships into mothballs) and some "experts" predicted that the market was tapped out. Thus, in 1977, when Cunard commissioned the brand new 17,000-ton (15,300 t) *Cunard Princess* (even the names were sounding more like resort hotels), they believed that she would probably be the last brand-new cruise ship ever built. This could not have been farther from the truth: there was simply a lull, a temporary downturn in the market. Within two years, the future would be brighter.

At about this time, Norwegian Caribbean Lines, who had a series of highly successful moderate-sized cruisers, looked into a revolutionary catamaran-style vessel, a vessel with twin

Holland America's *Nieuw Amsterdam,* completed in 1983, is one of the very finest contemporary cruise liners. Her modern exterior houses a unique interior: contemporary design and decor that is blended with $1 million in Dutch antiques. The decorative theme is Holland's colonial empire in North America and the Caribbean.

hulls of about 600 feet (180 m) in length and 150 feet (45 m) in width. They soon abandoned the idea, however, in favor of a "cruising superliner." To build such a ship would be too great a risk—instead company managers and engineers looked at existing tonnage to rehabilitate, such as the idle *United States, Michelangelo, Raffaello,* and *France.* The latter ship was the final choice. A deficit-ridden French Atlantic liner and occasional off-season cruise ship, she was often called a dinosaur, a white elephant destined for the scrap heap. Norwegian Caribbean Lines, much to the surprise of almost everyone else in the passenger ship business, saw the *France* quite differently. With an extensive remake, a thorough and complete cosmetic makeover, she could become the ideal cruise ship. There would be the inevitable economy measures: reducing the engine spaces, a cut in the size of the crew, and an increase in her total passenger capacity. But more importantly, on board went lavishly colorful lounges, bars, and casinos, and an altered theater that now presented full Broadway and Las Vegas productions. Recommissioned as the *Norway* in the spring of 1980, and after a total expenditure of some $130 million, she was not only the world's largest cruise liner, but one with some of the best entertainment on the seas—there were events from before breakfast to after midnight: basketball shoots, aerobic dancing, backgammon, bridge tournaments, fashion shows, and lectures on such topics as varied as handwriting analysis and stock investing. There was big band dance music in one bar and Latin disco in another. There was also a floor show, nightclub cabaret, bingo, more dancing, stargazing on deck, a first-run film and the inevitable midnight buffet.

The eighties saw an even larger, perhaps even more specialized breed of cruisers: Holland America's latest *Nieuw Amsterdam* and her sister *Noordam* blended contemporary décor with national antiques and treasures, the Italian-styled *Fairsky* had her own pizzeria and Britain's *Royal Princess* boasted over 150 cabins with their own terraces—apartments gone to sea! New levels and standards of luxury were even reached by the 4,200-ton (3,780 t) Norwegian cruise yachts, *Sea Goddess I* and *Sea Goddess II* of 1984–85. Eighty crew looked after 58 couples, all of them in suites outfitted with the conveniences of fully-stocked bars, television, VCR systems, and even stereos. The on board ambience was one of complete creature comfort: from cooking at a passenger's request to a stern platform for participating in watersports. The mostly one-week itineraries, priced from $4,600 by 1989, often called in at some of the world's most fabled

Because the *Norway*, the former *France*, is one of the largest cruise ships afloat, she carries two very special tenders. These were especially built for her (in 1980) and are large enough to be called *Little Norway I* and *Little Norway II*.

Broad lido decks are essential to today's sun-seeking cruise liners. Just about everything is brought to the poolside: entertainment, drinks, certainly food. Onboard the *Sea Goddess* (bottom), one of the most expensively-priced ships afloat, all cooking is done to special order. On the *Noordam* (right), there are midnight buffets on deck while the ship is moored in Juneau harbor.

ports: yacht harbors along the French Riviera, intimate bays in the Caribbean, remote anchorages in the East Indies. A new generation of passengers, too young even to recall the *Caronia,* were the market for this exceptional pair. Furthermore, since they became part of the Cunard Line in 1986, they are successors of sorts to that enormous fleet of mostly bygone Atlantic liners.

The cruise industry continues to boom, expanding to nearly $5 billion annually in the United States by 1989, primarily because of a quartet of factors. First, the cruise lines have made good friends with the airlines and together they offer travelers from all over the world easy and convenient ways to reach ports of embarkation. In a matter of hours, cruise passengers on these air-sea packages can be aboard a comfortable and inviting liner, housed in a thoughtfully equipped cabin (newer ships offer such touches as hairdryers and wall safes), sailing in warm weather waters. Second, cruising has become widely recognized as one of the best, if not the very best vacation value. Averaging $300 a day by the late 1980s, the relaxation and the rest are incomparable: unpacking only once, conveniently visiting ports of call, complete security and

pampering, the chance to make new friends (and perhaps even to find romance!), and the addition of few extra expenses. It has often been said that there are only two major decisions to be made each day on board a cruise ship: what to wear and what to order! Third, and although it has long since left prime-time television, the *Love Boat* series conveyed a very positive image and message to millions that cruising was fun for all—not just for the very old and the very rich. Many were prompted to take their very first sailing, usually a short trip, perhaps a weekend jaunt to the Bahamas, and then were "hooked"—cruising is very addictive and travelers often go again and again, usually on longer and more varied trips. The numbers continue to grow, and only five percent of the potential North American cruise market has even been tapped. Finally, the fourth factor is the array of on board diversions and recreations—the sports, the games, the shows. Daily programs keep passengers posted and, aboard one current, large liner, there were no less than eight different activities set for two to three o'clock in the afternoon. There's enrichment as well, since many passengers want more than bingo and cha-cha class— some liners boast lectures on astronomy, astrology, and aeronautics, on board resident authors and artists, cooking experts and fashion designers, and even a specialist on chocolate. Meryl Streep, Walter Cronkite, James A. Michener, and a former British prime minister have all lectured on cruise ships. Understandably, lectures on ocean liner history have increased in popularity—slide shows flickering on a theater screen give glimpses of the *Titanic* and *Queen*

Mary, those palm courts and carpeted kennels, the way it used to be. There have also been special-interest theme cruises: Hollywood nostalgia, Broadway theater, gardening, beauty and fitness, murder mystery, stop smoking, eclipse-viewing, whale-watching, ballroom dancing, and wine tasting.

A new peak was reached in early 1988, when Royal Caribbean Cruise Lines introduced the 73,200-ton (65,880 t) *Sovereign of the Seas,* the largest cruise ship ever and the fourth largest passenger ship ever built. A 14-deck hotel gone to sea, she has enough beds for over 2,600 guests. She was designed especially for the one-week eastern Caribbean trade out of Miami and, while solidly booked for her inaugural year, she is a prelude to two sister ships—one intended for the western Caribbean out of Miami and the other for San Juan sailings to the lower Caribbean. On board the *Sovereign,* there are 1,100 cabins, all featuring 12-channel television. She has 18 elevators, two pools and a full health center, 10 lounges, twin cinemas, two 650-seat restaurants, a complete conference/meeting center, and a lobby that rises five decks in height and includes balconies, complete with hanging foliage, as well as a pair of glass bubble elevators—Hyatt Regency on the high seas! A Royal Caribbean trademark from their very first ship 18 years earlier, the *Sovereign's* smokestack-cocktail lounge sits 14 decks above the sea, has a 360 degree view, and seats 200—cocktails in the sky!

Similar in competitive spirit to the great Atlantic liner rivalry of the 1930s are today's cruise ship owners who vie for different records and special distinctions. Carnival Cruise Lines is adding three mega-sister ships: the *Fantasy, Ecstasy,* and *Sensation.* At 70,000 tons (63,000 t) each, they too are aimed at the Florida–Caribbean trade. The first of them, the $200 million *Fantasy,* needing a marketing niche of her own (as did most of those earlier behemoths) lays claim to the largest entrance foyer ever to go to sea: six decks in height, with a changing atmosphere through sound and light systems, and capped by the largest glass dome ever fitted to a ship. It is appropriately called the "Grand Spectrum." Other features include a 1,300-seat Universe Lounge, Cleopatra's Bar in Egyptian motifs, the Electricity Discothèque, and the largest shipboard casino ever with 22 blackjack tables, 210 slots, four roulette stations, four dice tables, and a wheel of fortune.

When the 73,200-ton, 2,600-passenger *Sovereign of the Seas* had her debut in early 1988, it was rumored that she might be the last of the mega-liners. But the cruise industry continued to boom. Carnival Cruise Lines ordered a trio of 70,000 tonners—the *Fantasy, Ecstasy,* and *Sensation*—while Royal Caribbean responded with orders for *Sovereign II* and *Sovereign III,* with even larger capacities—over 3,000 passengers each.

Over two dozen additional cruise liners were on the boards by 1989–90. Most are intended for the Caribbean (still the most popular destination of all), but others will go to Alaska, Europe, and the Far East; and the smaller, more specialized vessels to Antarctica, Greenland, the Dalmatian Coast, and even Siberia. The Japanese are building their first major cruise ships, a trio of 49,000-tonners (44,100 t), which will include, among several restaurants, one that specializes in Oriental cuisine. Seabourn Cruise Lines, another Norwegian line, added its

second deluxe yacht, the 10,000-ton (9,000 t) *Seabourn Spirit,* which has nine decks and 140 crew members, but carries only 212 passengers, all of them in large suites. She and her sister, the *Seabourn Pride,* are currently the most expensively priced cruise ships ever, averaging $600 per day, double occupancy. Other fresh names added to ocean liner annals include *Crown Monarch, Star Princess, Royal Viking Sun, Oceanic Grace,* and *Crystal Harmony.*

The drawing boards for the 1990s and beyond reveal some of the biggest, most exceptional, and even extreme passenger liners (if they are to be accurately called liners), ever created. Studies reveal that passengers want bigger and bigger ships, and so the era of the 250,000-ton (225,000 t) 5,200-passenger *World City* may dawn. Originally known as the *Phoenix,* she was initially a project of Norwegian Caribbean Lines, but has now spun off separately and gradually increased to a total cost projection of $1 billion. Almost a quarter of a mile long and 100 yards wide, she would boast three separate hotel-like towers supported by a catamaran-style hull. Each would be styled as a separate resort, complete with palm trees, waterfalls, and quaint outdoor cafés. A quartet of 400-passenger super-tenders, or "day cruisers," would ferry guests to and from shore. The *World City* could berth only in the largest of harbors: New York, Miami, San Francisco. The on board entertainment possibilities would be virtually limitless: live theater, shipboard museums and galleries, bistros, discos, several cinemas, a 100,000-volume library, an exceptional conference center, a tennis court, at least a dozen pools, a half-mile jogging track, even a brokerage office, and a recreated Main Street with a village square and little shops. Estimates are that four German shipyards might build her, with possible delivery by 1993, and with operations divided: winters in the Caribbean, summers in Europe, and even some New York sailings.

Another scheme is the so-called *Rio Project,* an exceptionally wide design—250 feet (75 m)—but considerably shorter than expected length, only 722 feet (217 m). She would carry 3,500 passengers on weekly Caribbean trips and has already been dubbed the "cruise for everyone" vessel. Her appeal would be high volume, mass market—those passengers who want something new each day. Along with the casinos and lounges and discos, there would be such specialties as the Oilers' Bar, an amenity located alongside the lower-deck engine room and where passengers could view the engine room through glass and soundproof panels while sipping cocktails; a complete on board amusement park for the younger as well as the older travelers; and even a circular, internal rail system with stopovers on three decks. Once ordered, the $400 million *Rio* design could be completed in as little as two years.

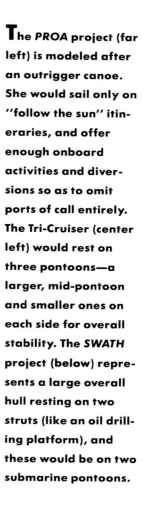

The *PROA* project (far left) is modeled after an outrigger canoe. She would sail only on "follow the sun" itineraries, and offer enough onboard activities and diversions so as to omit ports of call entirely. The Tri-Cruiser (center left) would rest on three pontoons—a larger, mid-pontoon and smaller ones on each side for overall stability. The *SWATH* project (below) represents a large overall hull resting on two struts (like an oil drilling platform), and these would be on two submarine pontoons.

The third possibility is the *Ultimate Dream,* a 116,000-tonner (104,400 t), 1,132 feet (340 m) in length and with space for 3,000 passengers. She would emphasize a more deluxe standard: every cabin would have a verandah and would measure a very spacious 205 square feet (18 m²). Also, there would be three ultra-luxurious penthouses, each measuring an unparalleled 860 square feet (77 m²). There would be eight different restaurants, each featuring a different cuisine; 12 pools; a tennis court; and a large shopping mall. She too would cruise the Caribbean, mostly on seven-day trips from Miami, and also a few months out of New York.

Other futuristic projects include an apartment-like tower of at least 12 levels mounted on an outrigger canoe-like pontoon hull, another multi-hulled design called the *Tri-Cruiser,* and the so-called *SWATH* cruiser (for Small Waterplane Area Twin Hull).

If such liners as the *World City,* the *Rio,* or the *Swath* come about, they will be, despite

Ship designers from the days of the four stackers and the palm verandas could not have envisioned the passenger ship ideas of the 1990s. Here, onboard the SWATH Project, a surfing platform is linked to the stern of the vessel by twin pipelike towing rods. Alternately, the platform can be used for sailboating and for small launch services.

their greatly changed appearances, purposes, and facilities, the true successors of the great age of the transoceanic liners. Who could have accurately envisioned the changes within a century—from the four-funnel, 14,000-ton, class-divided *Kaiser Wilhelm der Grosse* of 1897 to the possibility of the 250,000-ton, resort-like *World City*? Certainly, the story of ocean liners will continue. This book has captured the history of the great ocean liners—from the era of the Blue Ribbon and national rivalries, of potted palm first class and spartan steerage, of splendor and grace, ferocious Atlantic storms and fiery disasters along the New York City waterfront through the great transition from the age of the ocean crossing to the age of flight, and then the enormous expansion of leisure sailings and the era of sunshine cruising. Hopefully evocative, surely nostalgic, this book pays homage to one of the greatest moving objects to be made by man—the ocean liner.

SUGGESTIONS FOR FURTHER READING

Bonsor, N.R.P. *North Atlantic Seaway.* Prescot, Lancashire: T. Stephenson & Sons Limited, 1955.

Braynard, Frank O. *By Their Works Ye Shall Know Them.* New York: Gibbs & Cox Co., 1968.

Braynard, Frank O. *Lives of the Liners.* New York: Cornell Maritime Press, 1947.

Braynard, Frank, & Miller, William H. *Fifty Famous Liners.* Vols 1–3. Wellingborough, Northamptonshire: Patrick Stephens Ltd, 1982–87.

Braynard, Frank O. *The Big Ship: The Story of the SS United States.* Newport News, Virginia: Mariners Museum, 1981.

Brinnin, John Malcolm. *The Sway of the Grand Saloon.* New York: Delacorte Press, 1971.

Coleman, Terry. *The Liners.* New York: G.P. Putnam's Sons, 1977.

Kludas, Arnold. *Great Passenger Ships of the World,* Volumes 1–5. Cambridge, England: Patrick Stephens Ltd. 1972–76.

Maxtone-Graham, John. *The Only Way to Cross.* New York: The MacMillan Company, 1972.

Maxtone-Graham, John. *Liners to the Sun.* New York: The MacMillan Company, 1985.

PHOTO CREDITS

Courtesy Cunard Public Relations: 86 (all), 87 (all)

© FPG International/Collection of Everett Viez, FL: 65 (top left)

Courtesy Holland American Lines: 125 (top right, bottom right), 135

All photographs Suzanne Kaufman are courtesy Richard Faber Collection: 5 (all), 7, 14 (all), 19 (top right), 20 (top left), 29 (all), 30, 32, 34 (all), 36, 42, 44, 46 (all), 47, 48, 49 (all), 50, 52, 52-53, 54 (top right), 55, 56, 57 (all), 58 (bottom), 59 (top right, bottom right), 60, 61 (all), 62, 63 (all), 65 (top right), 66 (top right), 68 (left), 69 (all), 70, 78 (all), 81 (top right), 81 (bottom), 82 (all), 84 (top left), 90, 94 (bottom), 95, 97 (all), 102 (all), 103 (top right), 107 (top), 108, 110, 111 (all), 113 (all), 114, 116, 117 (bottom), 118, 119 (all), 126 (all)

© Allan Malschick: 130

Courtesy Collection of Bill Miller: 31, 120, 124, 125 (top left), 128, 129, 131, 132, 133 (all), 134 (all), 136 (all), 138

New York Public Library Picture Collection: 8, 10, 11, 12, 13, 15, 16, 18 (all), 19 (top left), 21, 22, 24, 26, 27, 31, 35, 51, 54 (top left), 58 (top), 59 (top right), 59 (top left), 64, 67, 68 (bottom), 74-75, 76, 77, 79, 81 (top left), 83, 92, 93 (all), 94 (top right), 96 (all), 98, 99, 100, 101, 103 (bottom), 104, 106, 107 (bottom), 109 (top), 117 (top left, top right), 123

HandColoring on page 22 by Melissa Dehncke

North Wind Picture Archive: 9

© PHOTOWORLD/FPG International: 28, 45, 72, 73, 80, 109 (bottom), 122

Courtesy Princess Cruise Lines: 120

© Shigekama: 84 (bottom)

INDEX

Page numbers in italics refer to captions, illustrations, and sidebars.